I'VE DECIDED

DECIDED

LIFE IS WHAT YOU MAKE IT

FRASER KENNEDY

WITH

JAMES WAGGOTT

I'VE DECIDED

EDITED BY
LISA CHANEY

Published by Vanity Rocks International, 2015
Copyright © Fraser Kennedy, 2015

First published in the United Kingdom in 2014
by Vanity Rocks International

Electronic edition published in 2016 by Vanity Rocks International

The White House, Chantry Lane, Bishopthorpe, York

A CIP catalogue record for this book is available from the British Library.

ISBN 978-0-9934507-0-9

Typeset by Ned Hoste
Printed in by CPI Group (UK)

Cover photo taken by Dave Humphreys www.davehumphreys.ca

2nd Edition
Gunning for the goal.

Preface

Hearing that Fraser's eyesight wasn't as good as it had been, I arrived at his house believing we'd talk about which writers he liked, and I'd read to him. For months afterwards it was a mystery to me how, far from discussing *reading*, I left having promised I'd help him *write* his memoir.

Fraser is a wizard at engaging people, at communicating. He's a natural; he loves it.

But Fraser can't take for granted the simple to and fro of ordinary conversation. For him, the act of listening, of speaking, is hard won. When you understand how much concentration and willpower he needs to exert here, you appreciate why his face is often serious. That's until you glimpse the sparkle in his eye and realise there's a sense of humour always at the ready.

When Fraser thinks something's funny, his eyes light up, he throws his head back – chuckling – and his face becomes an ear-to-ear smile. It's one of those smiles that persuades you everything is possible, that the world is a better place. And, as I've come to know him, I've realised it was this smile that provoked my reckless promise, to help him write his memoir.

Many months down the line, we began the long period of editing. Only then did Fraser and his friend James – as things turned out an inspired amanuensis – let slip they'd planned all along that I was to help with this book! We all laughed. They at how effective their hoodwinking had been; I at how clever they'd been, and all of us at how much enjoyment we'd had in the making of something that had sometimes been very difficult. Difficult, because Fraser and James were new to the game of writing (Essays for college, yes, but not a 'proper book'). Difficult, because, necessarily, their working methods were complex. But difficult, perhaps most of all, because we all had to work out how Fraser was going to express – at times from the depths – things he'd protected himself from articulating.

As a man of conviction and stamina, he's also an advocate of rationality, practicality and self-belief. Using these, his determination to take charge of his life and disability, rather than letting it take charge of him, is one of Fraser's outstanding qualities. It's also the crucial drive of this book. With the remarkable support he has generated – and is the first one to applaud – he's overcome some pretty outlandish odds and achieved many of his sometimes-crazy goals. Not least is the writing of this book.

In James, Fraser found the invaluable right hand man. James applied himself, with unfailing cheerfulness and goodwill, corroborating details, jogging Fraser's memory, provoking and encouraging talk about difficult subjects, and *always* writing everything down at breakneck speed.

Captured, as I was, to be part of Fraser and James's creative process, I've been privileged to observe their friendship. For all their blokiness and determination to appear tough, it's not only based on endless humour and great mutual respect, but also a degree of thoughtfulness about one another that's quite humbling. Without their friendship I'm not sure you'd now be reading this book.

When it came to one of my chief aims: liberating the slightly wooden writing style of those who are not accustomed to expressing themselves much on paper, their inevitable ease with each other was a plus. Over the months, we'd unpick rather formal pages that were nothing like the way Fraser and James actually speak. Gradually, their enthusiasm, hard work and constant humour, enabled them to bridge that strange gap between the written and spoken word. Fraser had found his writer's 'voice'. As a result, his book became more interesting and, finally, we were finished.

In the pages that follow, Fraser's mission is to share some of his hard won methods for overcoming major obstacles. To share them with those who may feel downhearted about their own situation. Without doubt, his mix of practicality, determination and self-belief, is a powerful and effective message. Yet, while it is for you the reader to judge Fraser's success in sharing his discoveries, as you read on I would ask you to bear in mind a vital element missing from his book.

This missing element is a subtle thing. It is a quality Fraser himself possesses but is unaware of. A quality that is impossible to avoid noticing when you meet him. Some would simply call it charisma. Charisma, yes, but there's more to it than that. Fraser radiates a kind of illumination, a light both colouring who he is and shining out toward others. Like his smile, this light helps persuade you that everything is possible, that the world is a better place.

Lisa Chaney, York.
June 2015

Foreword from Fraser

There have been a lot of firsts in writing this book, including writing this foreword. What I've realised is that forewords can't say much, for fear of ruining the rest. But what I can say is that writing this book has been an enjoyable process. Well, that's not quite right. It's been a necessary one, which became enjoyable.

Writing this foreword gives me the opportunity to do a little housekeeping. Firstly, all we tried to do was write a book that you might enjoy reading. I promise I won't be offended if you don't agree with the things I've said. I've realised I have but one person's perspective. What I offer is just a story really. Well, a story of stories. If you find it interesting, then that's absolutely fantastic. If you don't, that's fine too. After all, you can't love every book you buy.

The process of learning how to share all these perspectives, first demanded I understand what my perspectives actually are. I then had to express them in the written word. Here, I've had a rather enormous amount of help.

I offer thanks to Lisa Chaney for much of it. She is a prolific biographer and our executive editor. Lisa, hopefully we've produced a book that, in some way, you're as proud of as we are. If the book is interesting, then it's because you've made it so. If it isn't, then it wasn't for the lack of your efforts and patience. We would be surprised if you have to work with a pair of more hopeless amateurs in the future. If you do, then at least we will have helped you to know what to expect.

Lisa told us how to do it, helped us do it, and helped us fix it when we didn't do what she told us. It's impossibly better for her involvement. This includes letting us produce the book we wanted to write. This meant leaving the odd clunky bit in, and the occasional areas where we display our obvious ineptitude. When you come across these sections, please be sympathetic to Lisa's patience in getting the rest of it reading so much better.

One thing Lisa did without compromise was to improve the clarity and accuracy of the points we were trying to make. A phrase she likes, which I'll not forget, is 'Fraser, can you tell me what you're actually trying to say here?' Frequently, I would turn to Jimmy and he'd look back with a familiar 'no idea either' face. This invariably resulted in deletions and/or amendments so necessary it isn't funny.

The outcome is a book that has developed my thinking, and quite profoundly at times. In fact, it became clear that those around me sometimes understood how I go about things far better than I do myself.

Which brings me on to Jimmy. We first became friends at school; he was the babysitter's boyfriend. While she did the babysitting, we talked about FHM girls and Formula 1, while drinking copious amounts of Diet Coke. Nowadays, we talk about real girls, Formula 1 and skiing and Jimmy will likely be drinking a Bloody Mary. I'm still on the 'DC'. My knowledge of F1 team dynamics has always surpassed Jimmy's. I can rattle off the technical stuff, such as the engine suppliers and tyre compounds. This is because I possess a memory, something he doesn't. You can rely on him to lose all of his possessions at least once a day... his wallet, phone and keys are the normal culprits. In Whistler, he frequently loses so many hotel key cards that they have to tell the system we've checked out and back in again, so that it will give us more keys.

However, while *I* can remember things, Jimmy *understands* them. He has a calm, objective, rational, and logical view of the world. Crucially, he knows how to lucidly articulate and explain things *to me* – he's a clinical expert at popping the bad-logic bubbles that I find myself in. He's never afraid to tell me straight, no matter how much I don't want to hear it. Only Jimmy has this ability, but this is complemented by his thoughtfulness and attention to detail. Jimmy is always aware and mindful of the difficulties I face. This includes saving me from dull and pointless conversations... and boy can he talk, he's Wag the Blag.

One of Jimmy's qualities, which I didn't appreciate, is his patience. On several occasions we'd revisit a topic over and over, for weeks, until we got it. And when we did, he would clap his hands, do a hop, sit down, type furiously and then read something to me, which perfectly represented what we were just discussing. He's a Gatling gun writer.

I owe him the greatest. He's been the ideal partner for writing this book and I'd never have done it without his encouragement. This book is something I'm really proud of. In fact, I'm more proud of it than any of my other achievements (so far!). These words don't really do justice to the closeness and respect I have for Jimmy – but they'll have to do.

Additional thanks are due to a few other people. Firstly, to Dave Humphreys for his awesome cover picture. He's captured my 'blue steel' face perfectly (Jimmy says this is probably my sex-face too). Also, thanks to Steve Hopkins for his brilliant back-cover art. He assures me he made me look like Brad Pitt under the helmet. Steve's written a few words about the piece, which we've put at the back of the book. More thanks are due to Ben Turner (who took on much of the very-under-estimated formatting and layout work), and to Sarah Smelik and Ned Hoste (for getting the whole project across the line).

I stand by every word you're about to read, as I can't offer any more. I'll speak to you at the end of the book. I've some other things I want to say, but I'd prefer to share them with you on the other side... so to speak.

Enjoy my book, and thanks for the sit-ski.

Fraser

Foreword from James

I will keep this as short as possible, as I imagine you're more interested in reading Fraser's book. However, this is the only chance I have to speak to you directly, so it might be a little longer than you'd expect.

I'd like to share a couple of things I learnt about Fraser in helping to produce this book. The process tested our friendship at times, but not in a detrimental way. In the normal course of producing a chapter, Fraser and I would find ourselves debating a topic he or I felt we weren't being clear, candid, or helpful about in some way or another. This would help us get the point clear in our minds and then fairly represented on paper. At times, it's felt like every page has been soaked in these debates.

On many occasions, Fraser would end up doing a sort of half-sigh, quarter-roll of the eyes and then subtly (but visibly) compose himself. When I saw this I'd know it was time to stop, reassess the point I was really trying to make and approach things afresh. It would always break the spell and the thinking would flow again.

More often than not, it would turn out that I was mistaken but, on occasion, I was right. The point I'm making is that

Fraser's ability to absorb the naïve enthusiasm of his ill-trained amanuensis, and patiently get his point across, was exceptional. And on those occasions when he was mistaken, he showed incredible humility and grit in dealing with some pretty heavy topics. Fraser and I got better at managing these conflicts as the book progressed. So too did Fraser's ability and comfort to open up. This means that the book develops as you read it. We've left this element in as it shows the journey we went through in writing it.

Regardless, I can't imagine being as patient and willing to tackle harsh realities if I was in Fraser's position and someone was doing the same to me. In fact, I don't think I've met anybody who could have done this as well as him.

Fraser has also revealed a knack of being an astonishingly persuasive bastard, which I hadn't noticed before. Not in a pushy, gee-you-up way. More in a solid, glacial force of continued focus and polite persuasion kind of way. While I've juggled many other projects over the last eighteen months, the consistent end-of-the-evening or middle-of-the-night nagging thought has been, 'must do some book stuff'. Never did Fraser irritate or become (visibly) exasperated, he just applied a consistent and un-ignorable force that, ultimately, got us to the end. I'm very grateful to him for this; it's the reason this book is now in your hands.

The other thanks I offer are, of course, to Lisa Chaney. The role of translating Fraser's life stories into a book, via my decidedly C-grade English GCSE training, has tested me hugely. I suspect Lisa didn't quite realise what she had let herself in for when we submitted the first draft of the first chapter for review. Her composed and enthusiastic response was, and forever will be, one of the most expertly timed and elegantly executed white lies I've been on the end of. Working with Lisa has been an immensely enjoyable process. It's also given me some really useful skills, which I'll keep for the rest of my life. This emphatically includes the correct use of commas. I am now a low-ranking comma Nazi.

For me personally, writing this book represents one of those 'bucket list' goals, which many people say they'd like to achieve but rarely do. It gave Fraser and me a reason to hang out more and to talk in great depth about things that we'd probably skirted around over the years. It's given me a sense of validation for some choices I've made in my own life and it's also developed my thinking in many ways. Regarding *your* bucket-list, my advice is to consider going for the other items before going for this one! That said, I now think I don't ever want to *not* be writing a book. I've learnt to love it.

Something that perhaps doesn't overtly feature in the book, but I hope you'll notice is, what a kind, warm, thoughtful, loyal, good and *hard* man Fraser is. He has some extraordinary characteristics that I really hope are sufficiently demonstrated in these pages.

Those kind words mean that I can slap him now by adding that he can, occasionally, be vain beyond words, a bit naïve, and my goodness can he obsess over tiny details. Luckily that last 'flaw' marries nicely with my weakness in the opposite direction, which has resulted in innumerable 'Fraz-saves' as we wrote and reviewed the book.

To Fraser, I salute you. To Lisa, we thank you. To you the reader, thank you too for helping us. This has been, without doubt, the most inefficient way to purchase a sit-ski.

That's it from me.

Enjoy.

James

XVI | I've Decided

I've Decided

It starts here:

I decided I wanted a new sit-ski. It was that simple. So, a friend and I had the brilliant idea of writing a quick book, selling it to you and then going shopping. I'll cover what exactly a sit-ski is shortly, but for now we figured a few thousand dollars would do. We even had a slightly sneaky plan to reprint long emails that I sent on my travels as the lead-in to each chapter – providing thousands of words without having to write anything new. In a way, the sit-ski goal still stands. And, in reading this, you have helped me take a small step to making my goal a reality.

From my perspective, the job was done! But this book has evolved into something more than we intended at the beginning. We realised it wouldn't be fair to start with my travel emails and then pad out the rest of the pages with mindless babble and old photographs. Instead, I thought I'd take the opportunity to answer some of the questions others probably ask behind my back and a few have asked me to my face.

I suppose the real question is answered by the first sentence of this book – how does a guy like me end up asking a question like, 'How can I get a new sit-ski?' How did I reach this 'I've Decided' moment?

Let me tell you who I am.

Firstly, I'll describe myself with a bit of a positive spin. I'm a thirty-four-year-old man (but I believe I can pull off twenty-six) who keeps fit and wears trendy clothes. My mantra is 'Vanity Rocks'. I've toured North America, Europe, Africa and the Far East. Last year I went around the world and in every country I visited I never seemed short of friends. The truth is, I frequently have conversations with people who know me, but I have no idea who *they* are. This happens for two reasons: sometimes it's because I'm fairly well known (and recognisable); the other I'll explain later. I like to ski too... I prefer the largest ski area in North America as – like my clothes – I don't see why the best is anything but right for me. Girls-wise I'm best described as 'selective'.

I have a Bachelor's and Master's degree in Political Science: Conflict, Governance and Development. After my Master's, I was offered a job to join a project sponsored by the Australian Agency for International Development (AusAID). This was to investigate the effectiveness of political leaders and their influence on a country's development (or lack thereof). Through a mixture of good fortune and fluky timing, I found myself on a team investigating and advising the international community on how best to encourage socio-economic growth. I was invited to speak at a conference held at the World Bank Headquarters in Washington DC, close by the White House. My head was so big at the time it's lucky I managed to fit through the front doors. My boss, Adrian Leftwich, was the Chair at the conference and one of the leading figures in this field of work. He also became a good friend.

That's the self-aggrandising stuff out of the way, now let's do the hard luck bit.

I am profoundly physically disabled.

I've got Friedreich's Ataxia, a rare neurological degenerative disease of the central nervous system that rots away the myelin sheath of my nerves so that they work less each day (Jimmy just told me this and I didn't even know it!). For those who care, a primary cause of this breakdown is reduced mitochondrial function.

It started when I was four and I'm now thirty-four. Here's just a few of the joys I get to deal with:

- I'm totally wheelchair bound.
- Need twenty-four hour care with the help of live-in Personal Assistants (PAs).
- Had major back surgery, I have two metal rods fused with my spine.
- Had a collapsed lung during that stay in hospital.
- Had septicemia – it kills people 50% of the time.
- Have Type 1 diabetes (requiring a minimum of five injections a day).
- Fell into a diabetic coma.
- Wear an oxygen mask every evening, which makes me sound like a drunk Darth Vader.
- Have an enlarged heart – I have tachycardia and get episodes of atrial fibrillation (look it up if you're bothered).

- Numerous admissions to hospital.
- Can't write and haven't been able to since I was about twelve.
- My speech is badly slurred.
- Need help with everything involving physical movement or dexterity.
- My sight and hearing are both, well, far below the requirements for Top Gun.
- I wake up every morning stranded in my own bed.

Some might call mine a miserable existence. As a kid I had it all and then it was taken away, just when others around me took off into their lives. Poor little me.

This book is a stab at sharing how I think I've dealt with some of these challenges. Bridging the gap so that I can enjoy the good life I talked about earlier on. It's not intended to be a chronicle of my life. It's an attempt to share some interesting – maybe thought-provoking – things I've experienced.

I've tried to concentrate on '*how* I did it'. I mean I really don't care how I look out of this. I certainly don't want to make myself out to be some sort of self-congratulatory type (in other words a tosser). The truth is that millions of people the world over have it tougher than me and are in far worse circumstances. The fact that there are billions of people in the world is irrelevant. I'm more interested in sharing how I think I've done it. I think I've done enough of 'it' now to write a book about it. A short one.

We'll begin by telling you how I've done it.

Firstly, I'm not typing these words. I can't. So, I've teamed up with an old friend, James Waggott, who has co-written this book. By co-write, I mean type it all! (James: "Hi everyone!"). I call him Jimmy so will do for the rest of this book. I've also had loads of help from lots of other people who've mentored us through this process. They are acknowledged elsewhere.

I will make mistakes. I will learn a lot (In fact as we review the book I can tell you that I've learnt loads).

Remembering that I just said this is not a chronicle of my life – I'm going to start off with a short chronicle of my life.

I grew up as a normal kid in the 1980's to successful parents, Graham and Deirdre and one younger sister, Rebecca. In my early years we moved around but we eventually settled in York, North Yorkshire, UK. It was a very happy, loving and normal upbringing.

My dad tells people 'I am Fraser's creator'. This typifies his provocative personality. He thrives on making people feel uncomfortable. His default position is to challenge on anything – be it fashion choices, lifestyle, sexuality, political views or facial hair. Those that punch back often become good friends.

He channels this urge to provocation into business, which has made him very successful. He also uses it to be magnanimous. This makes him an unusual character. Annoying and nice, cutting and loving.

My mum trained as a nurse. She is generous and loved by everyone. Mum is the only person I know who has never said the word fuck.

When I was about four, my mum suspected there might be something wrong. I wasn't good at running and didn't like doing it for long. I was less steady and coordinated than I should have been. There followed a lengthy diagnosis process, which ended up in Great Ormond Street Hospital when I was ten. It was there that my parents found out I had Friedreich's

Ataxia, a degenerative disease named after the Scientist who identified it. At the same meeting the doctor asked my mum to fetch Rebecca, my seven-year old sister. As this is a genetic disorder, she needed checking as well. My mum remembers the doctor asking Rebecca to run up and down the corridor. Mum describes Rebecca's shoes as sounding like they were three sizes too big. Clompy. It turned out that Rebecca had Friedreich's Ataxia as well. Actually, mum had researched and diagnosed it a year earlier, but it took the doctors some time to catch up.

The significance of all this to our family was somewhat lost on my sister and me at the time. As soon as we got back in the car we asked to go to McDonalds, our diagnosis obviously hadn't put us off junk food.

My parents went on to have two more children. Sophie was born when I was eleven. She was only the second baby in the world to be prenatally screened for FA. Two years later my youngest sister Lucy was born. She too is FA free. She was only the *fourth* baby to be tested. Friedreich's Ataxia is *rare*.

Rebecca (Bex), is my three-and-a-half years younger sister. She has a kind heart. Her approach to life with FA is different from mine. Not better or worse, just different. Bex has a degree (and studied for a PHD) in Psychology. She's now completing a conversion into Law – clever girl. She has a sharp tongue like Dad. She can be venomously critical, but also jokey.

Sophie is twenty-two now and very much the 'it' girl. She's like a hybrid of Mum and Dad, gregarious, determined and thoughtful. She's doing a Fashion and Communication degree. She has the ability to spend money like water. As we write this she's doing so while studying in New York.

Lucy, the fourteen years younger baby... makes me feel very old. She has developed into a beautiful person with looks to match. Mum basically. She is currently studying American Studies at the University of East Anglia. I think she secretly wants to be in the 'O.C.' TV series.

When I started secondary school (Bootham School, York) the difference between me and the rest of my class was my slightly wobbly walk, corrective white trainers and not doing PE. I also had to use a portable word processor in class, as I wasn't good at writing.

In my first year at Bootham I didn't struggle but wasn't exceptional at anything either. I was reasonably popular as I'd known a few people from primary school and was generally comfortable getting stuck in socially. My parents were a huge help here as my house was always the coolest to go round to – basically we could do whatever we wanted! Being average was fine but I remember how chess club gave me a huge boost. It's all to do with a friend called Jonny Marlow. He was very brainy, top in everything academically. You'll understand why it made me feel very good to be better at chess than Jonny (well not better but I could certainly beat him occasionally). Better still I rejoiced in the fact that when we went to chess club after the holidays I was made Chess Captain and Jonny was my deputy! Looking back it was an early lesson in focussing on abilities rather than disabilities.

As the Friedreich's Ataxia (FA) worsened it became more difficult to walk, so at twelve I got my first wheelchair – mainly to cover the distances between different school blocks. I chose a neon yellow one. Back then, I could push the chair myself quite easily and enjoyed doing tricks. Arriving at form meeting one morning I decided to show off in front of the whole class by attempting a wheelie. You can probably guess already, it didn't work. I flipped the wheelchair over and lay on my back on the classroom floor with everyone staring in shock. I was embarrassed as hell and felt really, really uncool. My lesson here was, humility.

The wheelchair became a very ordinary thing for my friends and me. By the second year we'd developed a new extreme sport known as 'Death Runs'. This involved the dangerous activity of friends taking turns to reach the highest possible speed, with me still in the chair. We did everything you shouldn't do; high-speed turns and jumping off steps. I can remember the rush and that's something I've enjoyed in life ever since. Most of the runs were with Mooney, AKA Simon. This has now progressed to hurtling down the ski slopes of Whistler (in Canada), where he lives. Much more on this later. The 'Death Runs' at school came to an abrupt end when the chair dug in and threw me out. My leg hurt but I didn't think anything of it. The bell rang and I was still able to walk with Mooney's hand, as was usual then. That was until I tried to walk up the stairs. On the first tread my leg buckled and I fell in a heap on the floor in agony. This was doubly terrible as I burst into tears in front of a fifth-year girl. Not just any girl but the decidedly hot Sophie McGill. I was devastated. It turned out I'd hairline fractured my femur and I learnt another big lesson. I can push things too far... something I'm still working on!

There are two more points I'd like to make here. At the age of fourteen, I became very angry for a while. The reasons are pretty self-evident when I think about it, really. I was growing up, girls were getting hot, my mates were growing strong and I was growing weaker. John Morris, who was someone always looking for a laugh, and everyone liked to make fun of, was joking around and tried to say something funny. I turned to him and shouted "SHUT UP JOHN YOU BIG NOSED

BASTARD!" I got the laugh. The truth is, I remember feeling shameful during the class and I apologised to him later.

I tell this story because it's representative of where I was at the time. In a word, I was conflicted. My need to fit in and be popular was the same as any other fourteen year old, but I remember being provoked to anger, resentment, spitefulness and ridicule far too quickly. I had become immensely frustrated and the corresponding realisation of what was going on was being taken out on my friends. My idea of humour was about putting others down, and I'd go there quickly and aggressively. The thing was, I could see what I was doing and reflected on it.

I think I still have the ability to lash out but it's more under my control now. I only do it where I feel provoked by someone. As you'll see, the truth is that I don't like it when people say something is impossible. It's actually one of the many reasons I'm writing this book. There are a few people I'm looking forward to giving a copy to – *"Friggin' read this before we next meet!"*.

The second thing I'd like to share happened a week or two after the John Morris incident. There was a big party at Tom Sessions' house. It was his birthday in mid-June, so he'd invited about twenty-five friends to set up a festival-style camp at the end of his parents' garden. We all thought this was very cool. After watching a film we went outside to hang out in the tents. A while later everyone decided to go back inside to do something else. I decided to stay. My FA had progressed to such a degree that I couldn't have joined them again without their help, so I was committing to spending some time alone.

I dragged myself outside the tent, a few people were sleeping by this time but most had gone inside, so it was quiet, still, dark and peaceful. It was a clear night and I just lay there and started to think.

It was my epiphany.

I realised things were going to be different. There were going to be challenges and life wasn't going to pan out as I'd hoped. Looking back it was probably quite a mature bit of introspection for a hormone-laden fourteen-year-old. Maybe it was a function of FA's influence on my life, rather than any intellectual gift. I remember feeling a huge sense of conviction that I'd have to tackle everything head on and that things would be different. But FA *wasn't* going to stop me from doing everything I wanted to do.

It was at that moment that I changed my mindset. Obviously there were difficult things happening at school (wheelchair, sports, girls etc.), but I'd done a good job of not letting them affect me so far. I DECIDED that I wouldn't let FA define who I was. I would fight everything and do everything I wanted to do regardless. On reflection, this *decision* was my defining moment, hence the title of this book.

To colour this in a bit more... I'd like to tell you that, as far as I'm concerned, I *still* don't see many things wrong with me. I just need a hand to do things (including this book), things may be more difficult but I'll always find a way. This statement might appear to clash wildly with the list I gave earlier of what I have to deal with. Of course there's shit-loads wrong with me – some might call it a 'deliberate denial'. But from where I'm sitting it's about *choosing* the existence I want, and it works for me.

It's probably a good idea to stop here and get back to the purpose of this book. The 'how to do it' rather 'what I did'. I'm finding this introspection quite difficult. I don't think in terms of why much, I jump to the practical level. I'm not suggesting others do what I've done. But I strongly believe I've chosen to act on things. This has made my life more interesting and rewarding.

The following chapters attempt to explain some of those 'hows'. I'll try and give the best examples and keep it easy-going. But sometimes that just isn't possible. From time to time my stories of failing with girls will lighten the mood. I arrived at the themes working with Jimmy. Neither he nor I pretend to be the inventor of anything you read below but we hope that my perspectives on the life I've been given will be interesting for you.

We have settled on the following:

1. Looking Around You: ways of looking at things.

2. Cause and Effect: You react to the cards you are given or play them: let life control you or choose to control life.

3. Resource vs. Resourcefulness: Being resourceful in the face of resource limitation.

4. Control and Compromise, Fear and Failure.

5. Communication.

6. Tiny Little Steps: Small steps lead to huge changes.

7. Trust In Others: Putting your trust in others and saying 'yes'.

I know these points may sound abstract, esoteric or a bit odd. With luck they'll gradually make sense. If not, too late, you've already read my book!

Chapter 1

Looking Around You: ways of looking
at things.

In most respects I'm very ordinary. Like everyone else, I experience the challenges we face with school, work, relationships, interests, hobbies, money, stress, things not going to plan, depressing times, horrible shocks, unexpected great things, blind luck and bad luck.

I'm interested in the options we choose, the choices we're offered at every moment.

I think I'm fortunate in generally being able to see opportunities. It's something for which I give huge credit to my parents. My father was born into a working class family in a council estate in Glasgow and my mum to a comfortable middle-class family (also in Glasgow). Their relationship began at fifteen. It was deeply frowned upon by my mother's side and met with amazement from my father's. By the time I was diagnosed with FA they'd spent far more time together in life than apart. From my perspective, they made their future a reality despite conventional wisdom suggesting 'it'll never work'. The spirit in my family home has always been one of abundance, love, sincerity and fun. A sense of the brevity of life and the importance of living every day, is something I recall from my earliest years. I imagine this attitude was tested after my diagnosis, but I didn't notice. I was ten.

The fact that Rebecca and I both have Friedreich's Ataxia (FA) is nothing other than terribly bad luck. What my family has achieved, in spite of FA, proves how valuable this attitude to life has been. My parents have always had the ability to overcome challenges. Their marriage is based on it. The challenges I have faced and set myself have involved this at every stage. From my special trainers I wore in my first year at Bootham, to wheelchairs, my back operation, my recovery, going to the gym, travelling, paragliding and skiing. I've tried to face these challenges with as much Kennedy-family-spirit as possible.

I never accept the status quo. I don't accept difficulties well. Those who know me might be surprised to hear this. The truth is I'm not sure this has always been a good or a bad thing. I suspect the image I project is of someone who accepts a lot. I don't. I fight everything and only *then* accept what I've got. My wheelchair life, for example. My feet kept slipping off the footrest. Now they don't because I've modified my chair. My back started to twist again, so I got a new backrest to correct it. There's always a fight and then a solution. I have to accept a lot, but not without the fight.

This extends to my relationship with the disabled community. I don't really have one. I've never wanted to be part of it because, I have never accepted that I belong there.

Who hasn't met up with an old friend and been asked 'how's life going' and they've lied and said 'great thanks'? I do it all the time. In fact, you will see as you read on, I occasionally use these white lies to try and figure out who the frig I'm speaking to. I frequently have no idea. If we all talked totally openly about what's really going on in our heads/lives the world would be a pretty miserable place. Who we share our problems with is something everyone in their right mind chooses carefully. My group is so important to me that they even have a brand name! I cover these points in greater, occasionally humiliating, detail later on.

So, everyone has their problems. I believe that for most of the world's population, the issues ordinary people deal with on a daily basis put any we face in developed countries in the shade. But even in the developed world, *everyone* has problems that deserve consideration. They're all real to the individual and as far as I'm concerned, that's all that matters. Everyone has problems. I may have an unusual set of them, but I see my situation as no more than problems. This means that I don't feel any different from everyone else; I like thinking like this… I like it a lot.

For me, a good response to problems begins with 'Looking Around'.

If a friend described someone with FA it would not be a nice story. It would involve an unthinkable chain of events leaving that person with very little prospect of doing anything. Extreme sports would almost certainly be out of the question. They certainly wouldn't include paragliding or skiing.

I'll kick off with a paragliding story to explain my point here. When I was twenty-four, I travelled across southern Africa with some old friends from school. In South Africa I saw some people doing tandem jumps. I wanted to see if I could do it, I couldn't see any reason why not. We went up to the local paragliding school and I did a tandem flight. The thing is that paragliding is very straightforward and involves sitting down. You don't need huge mobility to do it. I was pretty well instantly hooked – like the playground Death Runs on steroids.

The leap from being stuck in my wheelchair to flying through the sky was a function of *looking* in the first place. I'll say that again. The leap began by Looking Around Me. When I meet people I'm frequently struck by how hard they sometimes find this simple, obvious point. I'm so struck in fact, that the thought's got it's own chapter. This one.

When people (and I'm including myself here) become frustrated, depressed or bored, it seems that they've become set in their ways. I notice how these include regretted career choices, love-to-hate TV chat, time-consuming hobbies, love affairs etc. These same people say to me how much they'd love to do something like paragliding but don't have the time, money or balls. I'd describe these views as resource-limited. They know they want to do it and they know they can do it, yet they're somehow paralysed by the current things they do.

The first step for me is to *really* look around, in ways that might appear ludicrous or over ambitious. You disregard *anything* that limits your ability to let yourself think freely and openly. You don't think in terms of the impossible or possible, but just let yourself think openly and freely about what it actually is that you *want*.

Once you get this clear in your head, then it's time to figure out how to do it and, crucially, whether it's a smart thing to do. It's this bit that, on my own admission, I don't always get right.

An example was my (brief) experience as a *solo*-paraglider. When I returned from South Africa, I set about finding a way to continue paragliding. It didn't take long to find a network of rather awesome people who run disabled paragliding courses in the Lake District, UK.

From my research, it had become clear that this wasn't something I could take on lightly. I learnt a lot from my three flights in South Africa. If I was to take full charge of a paraglider, I'd need to improve my strength, coordination and control of my upper body. Whilst FA massively reduces these abilities, you can still do *something* about it. I can train like anybody else, and in so doing improve my performance. The side-effect is the enjoyment of getting a regular 'deep burn' and improving my physique... vanity rocks. I actually spent about a year in the gym preparing myself. I go three to four times a week anyway, so I directed my training efforts to work the areas of my body that would give me the strength I believed I needed. More beefcake chat later.

I enrolled on a five-day course in the Lake District with a view to seeing how far I could go with paragliding. There was quite a lot of book-work to cover, including understanding the physics of paragliders, airflow, cloud formation and thermals. Jocky, a seriously cool dude, was the main trainer and we took several flights together in a 'disabled rig', a tandem-seated tub with wheels (www.jockysanderson.com).

On these flights I went from being a pure passenger to more or less flying unaided but with Jocky there for back-up. After several more flights I flew solo on Jocky's recommendation; he'd given me the option. The first flight was wonderful and smooth. It was thrilling rather than terrifying, as I had radio contact with Jocky. When I was going wrong he was there to advise me, just like on the tandem flights.

I now have a license and useful form of ID! Jimmy finds it amusing how, despite the fact that I never actually need it, I like to keep it in the front of my wallet. He even used it as proof of ID for me in Whistler once.

Then there was the flight a year later. Ironically, this was preceded by a call from my mum. She wanted to know how things were going and I explained to her that I couldn't really talk at the moment, as I was about to fly off a mountain. We'd have to talk later. I didn't need to see her to know the blood had drained from her face as her concern for my safety blasted through the handset until, I just said, "Great Mum, speak to you in a bit," and passed the phone back to my friend Matty... Mum was in full flow as I did so.

What did she know? Quite a lot as it turned out.

We hadn't realised that my limited core strength meant I was less stable than I needed to be. It's important to keep your weight central in paragliding, as your weight distribution plays a key role in determining which way you go. Shortly after take off my upper body shifted to the left. So, as I pulled the left and right steering cords I couldn't turn left and right, just left and more left.

I crashed into a stone wall.

That's not strictly true. I ended *up* crashing into a stone wall. This was after landing heavily in a field of cattle, crashing through a bramble bush, off a tree, through a stream and into said wall. I did miss a couple of cows though, I remember the Doppler shift of their moo's as I screamed past them.

Looking Around Me only got me so far – and then into that wall. In not accepting my limitations, I was able to look around me. This is what got me into the sky. Unfortunately, I lost track of my limitations.

I will continue to push myself, but I know I can go too far.

I've gone back to tandem flying most recently in New Zealand. It was epic. By sticking to flying with someone else I'm able to take off from much higher places. It actually allows me to fly *more* independently, as I have the same level of control as before. When my stability gets in the way the instructor takes over, I centre myself and then it's 100% me again. This sort of collaboration is something you'll hear a lot about in the coming chapters.

Another example of Looking Around Me is my love affair with skiing, I've been every year for the last eight. It's as close to 'my purpose' as anything I've done. I love it. There's a peculiar grace involved in the annual melting of the snow. Otherwise I'd be on the bankruptcy register by now.

When I ski I use a 'sit-ski', a hybrid of technologies borrowed from skiing, high-tech mountain bikes and snowmobiles. I sit in a similar position to an F1 driver. Sitting upright with my legs out in front of me, my entire body is strapped to the sit-ski so that we are essentially one piece of kit. I hold two 'outriggers'. These are short poles with tiny skis attached, that I use a bit like balancing beams to control the side-to-side movement of the sit-ski.

Once underway and over about 10mph the sit-ski behaves rather like a bicycle, it wants to stay upright and leaning one way or the other causes the sit-ski to tip and turn. These superb bits of engineering allow those with limited mobility to ski as freely as possible but in a controlled and (relatively) safe way. I ski in Canada where the pistes are wide and the skills and resources are world-class. Canadian culture is outstanding in terms of the willingness and conviction with which it supports people like me taking on these extreme sports. It's one of the better places in the world to be in a wheelchair.

I ski collaboratively, rather like the way I'm writing this book. I sit in the sit-ski and am responsible for using my outriggers to transfer my weight, depending on what direction we want to take and the steepness of the pitch. A shallow slope needs gentle lefts and rights to control speed and avoid others. A steeper pitch requires much deeper and more dramatic turns to maintain a controlled speed. My instructors ski directly behind me and hold onto a handle located behind my head. They are there to assist me when I need it, *not* to take me for a ride. If I go into a turn too lightly, they push the handle down to deepen the turn angle. If I go in too deep they lift the handle so we turn less tightly (this is known as 'thumbing'). The goal is for them to ski passively behind me, so that I am in full control.

How well I do depends on the terrain, steepness, snow conditions and my performance on the day. I like to think I never make mistakes, but I frequently do. I'm constantly learning, just like everyone else on the mountain. From the kids on the nursery slopes to the fearless adrenalin junkies, I understand and fully endorse the addiction. We're all doing the same thing, developing our skills with every run so as to ski better and better. It's interesting to understand how something so essentially pointless means so much to so many people. Going up a mountain in order to come down again doesn't actually achieve anything, but the meanings we weave into it are absolutely wonderful.

It was a ski trip four years ago that I'd like to talk about now. My instructor was James Peters, a local ski professional who helps disabled people to ski in winter. He's my co-star on the front cover. In summer he helps badly dressed men and women hit balls with a stick in order to walk to said ball and hit it again. Golf. It's a game I'm truly grateful I don't have the capacity to play. It's clearly shit.

Despite this, James is an incredibly good sit-ski instructor. Each instructor has their own particular style. I love the variety. One instructor might prefer to stick to shallower slopes where we work on the technical aspects of my skiing. Another might prefer to go faster where, at times, we hit over 100kph. On these runs my contribution has to be pared back a bit for safety. From my perspective, the best instructor does everything but has a slight preference for going as fast as possible. This man is a six-foot-three moustachioed ex-fire-chief called Gil, for whom I have a worshiping admiration.

James's style of instruction is best described as fast, with a side-order of 'pushing it' in terms of terrain. Of all the big chances I've taken, probably 60% of them have been with James. By 'chance' I mean when the risk envelope is pushed. I go fast with lots of other instructors, particularly Gil, who is fast as hell – he's the fastest – but the risks he takes are expertly judged. Of all the big crashes I've had 85% of them have been with James too! You get the idea. His style, quite understandably, frequently landed him in trouble with the ski-school management (Whistler Adaptive Ski Program - WASP). But that's their problem, not ours! We get on great.

On a ski day with James in 2010, we were heading back to the main on-mountain facility for lunch and to warm up. There was a familiar return trail that we'd skied dozens of times before. As skiers will know, there are often opportunities to cut the corners off a zigzagging piste and find a steeper, less skied and more challenging pitch. James suggested we do this that day, as there'd been a fresh dump of snow. My response as usual was, "Yes, let's go for it." Jimmy knew the route and went ahead to watch, and catch his breath.

James and I crashed. Badly.

We rolled the sit-ski. Meaning, we rolled over.

It was a mix of an awkward turn, me not getting my weight across and an equipment failure at just the wrong time. Something came off the sit-ski. A ski! We had rolled the sit-ski before and, as usual, there were no injuries other than our pride. I remember that the volunteers helping were particularly hot that day, which always helps. It was when we were back at the 'Roundhouse' facility for lunch that I – and I later discovered the instructors too – realised Jimmy was unusually quiet. He doesn't exactly suffer from being tongue-tied, 'Jimmy-jabber' is more common. When the instructors and volunteers went to get their food he pulled my chair towards him and said he had something to talk to me about at dinner. My response was, "Cool, let's go ski."

Dinner chat later... Jimmy had seen me crash lots and lots of times, it's a part of skiing that everyone who skis or snowboards will understand. He explained to me what he'd seen and how it was something more serious this time. From his position he watched us flip over and saw the speed of rotation and the angle at which we hit the slope. As far as he was concerned, I was a few inches off breaking my neck. By the way he was talking, I knew he wasn't joking. He explained that when he'd seen me roll before it was just that, a smooth roll. On this occasion, the sit-ski had dug in and bucked up in the air before we began to roll. He described how far around we got before hitting the slope. If we'd rotated ten or fifteen degrees less, my head would have dug straight in with the full weight of the sit-ski on top. Instead, we had rotated just enough for the sit-ski and instructor to tumble over me and vice versa (he's getting sweaty palms as he types this).

Jimmy is an unusually good communicator and I think he'd spent some time rehearsing his lines, so that this chat wouldn't be 'an awesome story to boast about at après'. He was deadly serious and was not happy at all, again fairly rare behaviour. He asked me to consider *why* we were in Whistler, what my goals regarding skiing were and what the consequences of a serious injury would be. He asked me to consider what life would be like as a *tetraplegic* with Friedreich's Ataxia.

At this point I made a big mistake. I disagreed with Jimmy. This has only happened twice. He had already shared his feelings with James the instructor on a lift when I wasn't next to him. I was worried that James would heed his concerns and reduce the speed and steepness of pitches we skied. Moreover, I'd lose the reputation I had as someone who always pushes their limits. That evening, I gave Jimmy strict instructions to take back what he'd said. I didn't think that anything should or would change. As far as I was concerned, the truth was that a crash like that could happen anytime, anywhere, and I understood the risks I was taking. My response, to quote Wayne's World, was 'game on'. In hindsight, I realise I was at fault. I'm not precious about my own safety. *But* this crash could have changed the life of several others, most notably James the instructor, Jimmy, Mum, Dad and my friends. There would also have been the practical details of learning to adapt to a totally new set of challenges, which would be, I concede, pretty horrendous.

I also learned later that one of the volunteers, also a great friend of mine, Desirée Patterson (a wonderful photographer, www.desireepatterson.com), had spoken with James after speaking with Jimmy. She had sat James down and said, "Whose limits are you pushing James? Yours or Fraser's?" As we ski collaboratively it was a really insightful and intelligent point. Apparently James took what she said on board... we still do crazy shit, but not fucking stupid shit.

The crash was one of my own making. If I consider that I always say 'yes', with the logic that I can put my faith in others, then a loop is created where others put more and more faith in me. My arrogance and blind belief that this was correct, led me to have a disagreement with one of my closest friends who was trying to look after my safety. I didn't take responsibility for my actions… I lost my way.

The event passed into history and has never really been spoken of with James or the WASP team since. Something I've learnt through having FA is, to take responsibility, not to blame others, and to show humility. Skiing is inherently dangerous and these are the 'rules of the game'. It's how I play it that matters. Like I said, it's amazing how something so essentially pointless can give someone such lessons in life.

Several things are going on here.

It was only by *looking* in the first place, that I found myself paragliding or skiing. If I'd read the book on being disabled, or followed the path I was expected to take, without looking around for new opportunities, then I would have never done those things. It begins with looking around to see what is *really* available to us in life. I take no credit for this. It is a value instilled in me by my parents.

It's clear that in order to successfully paraglide or ski, I first need to put my trust in other people. A lot of it too. The thing that I've realised, is that I generally I don't think you can ever put too much trust in others. The challenge is to ensure that I'm really *trusting* them, rather than having blind faith in them. I'll explain.

I'm not bothered about dictionary definitions here… just my own. For me, I see trust as a *mutual* process. The trust others put in me is a function of the trust I put in them. It's a two-way thing and needs checks and balances. Problems arise when trust turns into faith, I call it blind faith. It's here that things get a bit hairy. For the most part people find putting trust in others difficult. But because my whole life is built on trust in others and I like doing extreme stuff, the consequences of blind faith have sometimes been challenging for me. If you put blind faith in somebody doing something banal, like painting your toenails, then the worst that could happen is badly painted toenails. If it's to do with something more serious, like skiing, paragliding (or cutting my hair for that matter), then the consequences of mistakes here are in another league. Much of this book is about just this.

Time for a list... areas where I put my trust in others:

- Skiing.
- Paragliding.
- Travelling and especially putting me on the right plane.
- Not slicing my face when shaving (Garritt has challenges here).
- Diabetes insulin injections.
- Choosing matching socks.
- Handling the wheelchair up and down stairs or on ice/ through snow (Riva struggles here).
- Not poisoning me.
- Driving.
- Navigating anywhere (my crazy eyes make map-reading a ball-ache and jeopardises friendships).
- Book writing.
- Advising me that a white shirt isn't the best choice when going out for a meal.
- Filling in forms.
- Winding my watch and setting it to the correct time – Dylan likes to set it ten minutes slow.
- Writing birthday card messages.

- Not burning my mouth off with hot tea.
- Gym training, specifically not dropping 20kg weights on my face or dropping me.
- Styling my precious hair.

Therefore, I put trust in others quite a lot.

From those paragliding and skiing stories, I came away with no more than a hard-looking Joker-off-Batman scratch on one cheek (from the bramble bush) and a sore neck from flipping the sit-ski. The implications for those who put their faith in me were far wider. I made others feel bad, damaged their equipment, called their professionalism into question, created a pile of administrative and safety bullshit, and nearly gave my mum two heart attacks. So, it was my fault. It was my fault for saying 'yes', when I should have said 'no'. The truth is that *perhaps* these situations occur in my life a little more frequently than they should. If you put blind faith in others there's an inherent danger that they might put too much faith in you. For example, if the ski instructor asks me if I want to go faster and I keep saying yes, then sooner or later we'll both end up going far faster than we should. I now take full responsibility for what happened. It is important to do these things. 'Responsibility' and the value of 'yes' are covered in much more detail in later chapters.

Please understand that the fun and dangerous situations I've described above are not the lessons I'm trying to share. The lesson is something far more important – it's the importance of Looking Around You. The lesson is simple, *look around you for opportunities in life, there are always possibilities.* By rejecting convention and preconceptions, I've achieved a Master's degree, an interesting career, and success in extreme sports. I've travelled widely, have loads of close friends and am writing this book. But I still have bad girl chat!

I don't see these things as 'achievements' per se. My confidence doesn't stem from others' opinions of me. I'm actually much more selfish than that and would suggest you consider this for yourself. I've only done what I want to do. In my humble opinion, there are normally far more opportunities at your fingertips if you only choose to look for them. They are often staring you in the face.

At first, this *looking* does need a slightly healthy degree of *inanity* – an ability to think ludicrously, just to see what's out there. Why not?, who says?, and screw it, take the plunge. I don't want to be preachy, but it works for me.

Girls time. I have famously 'bad chat' with girls. In addition, I also have a few other issues that fit nicely into this 'Looking Around You' chapter. The main problem I occasionally have, is being able to see or hear them.

Here's an example…

When I was twenty-one I travelled around America with some friends: Rory, Tom, George, Olly, Alex and Jimmy – it was a collective gift from all the guests at my twenty-first birthday party. I'd asked people to make a donation to charity as I didn't really want anything and I'm known for being a nightmare about presents. Instead, my generous and image-boosting plot was hijacked. Claire Taylor, a friend of my parents, secretly contacted all of the guests and invited them to make contributions to a pot for me to go travelling with. It was perfect. I got the best present imaginable and looked cool in the process.

(My main focus on the day of the party was a speech I was

to give with Jimmy. We'd practised for ages and probably only did a passible job, but we felt like we were going on CNN. So, the travel-fund present was a huge surprise, it floored me.)

The trip basically consisted of friends and me travelling all over the place having fun. We ended up visiting New York City, Washington DC and Vancouver, where we hired an RV to drive to San Francisco via Seattle and Yosemite National Park. In San Francisco we swapped the RV for a car to drive to LA, via Napa Valley and Highway 101. Obviously, we ended up in Sin City, Las Vegas, to get hammered and reckless. There's a book in itself here, but for the sake of Jimmy's reputation I'll hold back. But it did involve armed security guards... oh and we broke Rory too.

When I was in Seattle with Tom and Rory, we'd decided to meet up with one of Tom's friends, Darren. He was (and probably still is) a smooth, suave, funky, whacky type, with a side order of nerd appeal. Men want to be him and women want to be with him.

Jimmy is friends with the owners of a boutique hotel in Seattle - the 'Inn at the Market' - who kindly offered us free rooms for a couple of nights. It was probably the best hotel I've ever stayed in. This was especially the case, because we arrived from Vancouver after three days in an RV. Driving through Seattle centre was pretty hairy. I was fine, but Rory was definitely sweating. We got to the hotel and walked in, it was very suave, quiet and classy. Rory wasn't, after the traumatic drive through town. As we checked in the manager said we had two rooms, so we were chuffed. Looking like bums and with Rory smelling fruity, we got the key cards and went to the lift, passing other guests with their Louis Vuitton bags. We were maybe a bit out of place, with trainers, plastic carrier bags and rucksacks.

My room was massive, with a huge bed and bathroom and *two* PlayStations. It was 2002. I figured Tom and Rory would be slumming it in a smaller room. I generally win in these situations. They got room 601 on the top floor. We found two doors, 601a and 601b. Rory tried the first and it opened. He wheeled me into a big lounge with panoramic views of Seattle. We turned the corner and there was a big kitchen too. This was great, except there didn't appear to be any bedrooms. We shortly learned that there was an *upstairs*. I got a room and they got the best suite in the hotel – *bastards*.

The scene is now set. Back to girls (Actually, just skip this bit Grandma...).

Cool bastard Darren came round to the suite with a friend. Both were amazed. That night, we went out in Seattle and, as usual, I was being aloof and not paying much attention. I do tend to drift off now and then. Darren's ex-girlfriend got us VIP entry into the club where she worked. I was looking about and sort of taking it all in, sort of drifting, I was tired after the sweaty-Rory-driving and it was dark.

I snapped out of it to calls of, "Fraz, FRAZ, meet *Brie*." I turned around, 'Holy shit'. Brie was twenty-six, an ex-Playboy model and drop-dead gorgeous. She was very cool too. Trust friggin' Darren to have a Playboy model as an ex... Damn him!

After a while, Tom and I headed for the bathroom. We were crossing the dance floor when Brie stopped us and started dancing with me in the chair. I pulled Tom and said, "Tom, pissing can wait... screw the loo!". Brie had a knitted top on and was more or less lap-dancing with me... AWESOME.

The song changes...

"It's getting hot in here, so take off all your clothes,". Her

top starts coming up as the song progressed – 'this is heaven' – and she straddles me as the chorus kicks in. There I was in the middle of the club with a stunning girl and her top was completely off. I remember looking over at Tom. His jaw had hit the ground and he was shaking his head in slow and envious disbelief. Then there were *more girls*. Another girl who we didn't know (very hot also) came over and started taking *her* top off. Tom thought I was the luckiest man alive. I thought, 'FUCK YEAH I HAVE ARRIVED AND BELONG IN SEATTLE!'

Later, we go home to the hotel. Tom was giving me a hand to bed.

Tom: "What the hell happened tonight? You do realise what happened don't you?"
Me: "Yeah, of course."
Tom: "What did you actually *see* Fraz?" Tom knows me well.
Me: "It was very dark Tom... I think I saw boobs. Or more silhouettes of boobs."
The truth is, I'm not entirely sure that I even saw silhouettes (I didn't Mum, really).
Tom's jealousy turned to exasperation: "SILHOUETTES?!"
To this day it is a running joke - twelve years and counting, I don't see it going away.
It shows me that maybe I need to improve on being able to look around. The lesson I learnt about humility when I tipped my chair in class has prepared me, though these incidents are *much* more fun.
A lot of the problems I have with girls are the fault of Friedreich's Ataxia. Notwithstanding the challenges wheelchair users have in attracting partners, on a practical level my

sight is crap in low light and my hearing is terrible in noisy environments. The point is that it's still my responsibility to work on these things. Looking Around Me is a particular challenge I have and the fact I'm crap at it to start with, makes it all the more my responsibility to work on it.

There are parallels with others facing challenges. Someone lacking confidence would probably be better served by working on it than avoiding it. Someone with a predisposition to putting on weight ought to focus more on the issue not less.

Taking this to the extreme. Why don't we just say it's *all* our responsibility, *particularly* when it isn't our fault.

Chapter 2

Cause and Effect... You react to the cards you are given or play them: life controls you or you choose to control life.

I'm still finding this introspective stuff difficult.

In the course of our meetings to get the notes down, I've realised I don't think in terms of 'why' much, I just jump to the practical level. While I've been telling you my stories, Jimmy has consistently been asking me "Fraz, you need to get the 'why?' down. Otherwise you're at risk of just talking about yourself – you've said that's exactly what you didn't want us to do". Actually, I think Lisa, our editor in charge, is saying the same, albeit slightly differently. I've realised that I'm pretty crap at 'why', but I'll get over it.

I've not really had to worry about why's. I focus on a practical level and, in truth, I'm fairly selfish, sorry about that, Mum. Like everyone, I need to be respected. Like everyone, I also need to have self-respect. But that doesn't mean that what

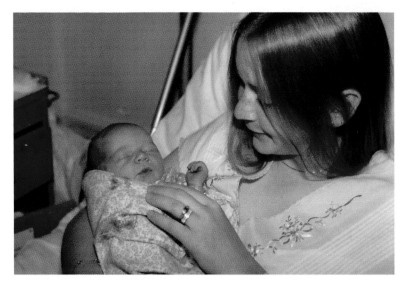

A new dawn, a new beginning… The arrival!

Aged 4: Pre-diagnosis, but post-need-for-speed

With my sister Rebecca. Bright colours were clearly in fashion. Aged 7 and 5.

Hanging out with Matty, pre-wheelchair, just. My journey into fashion hasn't always been a smooth one.

First ever ski trip at 14. Note the primitive sit-ski, and Jimmy's horrendous fashion sense. At least the sit-skis have improved.

Clockwise from left: having a family Mexican meal Dad, Aunt Vivienne, Mum, Aunt Gillian, John Morris and a very thin, 6-stone 16-year-old Fraser, post back surgery.

Public speaking genesis. Jimmy interviews me on my 21st birthday.

Sisters Sophie (9) and Lucy (7) undertake vital admin at my 21st birthday.

Bachelor's degree at aged 21, with Jegan.

Bachelor's degree with my family. About an hour later,
I was very drunk.

Paragliding genesis when I was 23, Cape Town, South Africa.

Aged 21 and praying at
the church of high-fashion.
Rodeo Drive, Beverly Hills.

Annabel (23), Alex (22), me (23) and George (22) on tour in a very hot Africa.

Easy Rider. Dessert riding aged 23 with Alex, Namibia, Africa.

Paragliding safety brief when I was 28. This was about an hour before I crashed.

This was minutes before.

Commuting in my sit-ski. Photo taken by Desirée Patterson www.desireepatterson.com

Skiing at 29 with Gil, pretty much my perfect day out. Photo taken by Dave Humphreys www.davehumphreys.ca

James and I skiing together. 15 minutes before my roll. Photo taken by Desirée Patterson www.desireepatterson.com

A perfect day. Photo taken by Desirée Patterson www.desireepatterson.com

Ready to shred the pow...the Whistler look.

I do is initiated by my need for respect, it comes as a pleasant by-product. I don't do what I do to look cool, I do it because I've decided to do it.

Anyway, back in the room.

In the first chapter, I talked about how I've generally found that pushing limits starts with broadening your perspectives. It is so simple that you'd think it'd be obvious. But I just stumbled into it. What *can* you do? What are the real options available to you? Not what options aren't.

This nicely introduces this chapter, which we've decided to call Cause and Effect. I hope it will make some sense.

When I was sixteen, I had to make a decision that, amongst other things, gave me a 25% chance of dying. One of the problems associated with FA is a severe scoliosis. This is when your spine turns into an 'S' shape and your whole body becomes twisted. By the age of eleven my back had already begun to bend and by the time I was fifteen it was so bad that the bottom of my rib cage was grating against my pelvis. Try this yourself and you'll get some idea.

There are two treatments for this – leave it or fix it.

In the 'leave it' corner is the certainty of survival. Amongst the dozens of problems FA gives you, one is an enlarged heart and weaker cardiovascular system. In medical terms, you're old before your time and the risks of surgery are amplified, rather like it is for old people. I'm allergic to this sort of logic, as listening to it sends me directly to a place of acceptance. And acceptance, in my book, more often than not leads to shit outcomes. But I'll not get ahead of myself here.

In the 'fix it' corner, was a straight back. This meant my appearance would be that of a straight-sitting man and the avoidance of scoliosis complications. This would include having increasingly complicated wheelchairs and adaptations to my home.

Being brutally honest, I didn't care about anything at fifteen other than how good I looked. Vanity is something I've been known for since I was young. As my mates grew stronger and the girls grew boobs, and learnt to wear less, I became intensely focused on my appearance. I hated my scoliosis and it needed correcting.

The operation, as many will already know, is pretty major. It involves a surgeon making an incision from the top of your neck down to the top of your bum. Your twisted back is pulled straight and then two metal rods, known as Harrington Rods, are fused either side of your spine. My consultant was Professor Dickson at St James' hospital in Leeds. We called him 'The Big Dick' - he must have been six-foot-four and I remember him having massive hands. My mum had known about this option since my diagnosis and we'd discussed it for a year prior to meeting him. The Big Dick explained the operation, that I would be in hospital for five to six weeks, and that the recovery period would be months not weeks. Added to all that was that statistic – 25% chance of it being fatal.

I'm not being macho when I say I didn't hesitate and said, "Yes, lets do it.". My confidence was reinforced by a pile of testimonials about the Harrington Rods operation that I'd printed from the Internet. I brought them to the consultation. I wanted to demonstrate how seriously I'd taken my decision. In my mind, I was being clear about what I needed to do. I always aim to take challenges head on. Naïve? Foolish? Probably a bit of both. Incidentally, this hasn't changed. However foolish or naïve it might be, whatever the challenge, I prefer to find the immediate solution and take action decisively.

I suppose really I was just being a sixteen-year-old. It's not an age known for giving *full* consideration to the consequences of one's actions. The simple truth is that I didn't think it through properly. I thought about it as four or five weeks in hospital and then the whole of the summer to enjoy. As it turned out, the complete recovery period was eight years, and the first two were a real challenge. The operation date was set for three days after my GCSE's finished.

The day I went in, they showed me the high dependency ward. I remember thinking, "Oh my god, what have I let myself in for?". Four beds, tubes, drips and beeps everywhere. Only then did it dawn on me how big a deal it was. My poor mum had been quite aware of what I was letting myself in for when the Big Dick said 25%. I still remember her gasp to this day.

Nonetheless, my mum and dad, but especially my mum, have always fully supported me in what I've chosen to do. Dad is always supportive in the end, but he doesn't work by taking risks. He works by thinking everything through. But it's Mum who generally supports me *first*, because she's more of a risk taker. For example, when I suggested skiing for the first time, Dad was very cautious and precious about my safety. Mum was much more comfortable in saying, "Go for it."

The operation itself went pretty well, although not without complications. It was eleven hours in total. One complication was that my blood loss was high, seventeen units. This meant that by the end every drop of blood in my body was other people's. The urgency to finish the operation meant that when they found one of the rods was cut to the wrong length, they decided to bend it at the top. I had no say in this... the cheek.

When I first arrived in the High Dependency Unit after the

operation, my mum was shocked to see that I'd grown three to four inches in height (I like to think I'd gone from Tom Cruise to Brad Pitt). Throughout my time in hospital, she kept vigil by me. I'm talking 24/7, with a camp bed at my bedside. She was there for twenty-eight days, save for one night when my aunt Gillian stepped in. We joke today that Mum only went home to make sure the house was being kept in order in her absence. Mum reassured me my grandparents were doing an excellent job holding the fort. I was so weak that I didn't really know what was going on. By way of example, I mumbled that I wanted to watch the Grand Prix. I was obsessed, and still am somewhat, so they found a TV and put it next to the bed. I was conscious for the start but soon drifted off... I woke later and watched the end. However, in my mind, I thought I'd watched the first Grand Prix, fallen back into a delirium for a week and then watched *another* one. In the hour that I was asleep I'd become convinced that a week had passed. I was seriously messed up.

While at my bedside in the High Dependency Unit, my mum noticed I was breathing 'abdominally'. She was told it was nothing and to go home for a much-needed break, as my dad had come to the hospital for a day shift. Mum hadn't been home long when the phone rang. It was Dad calling to reassure her that everything was OK. This included a passing comment that my lung had collapsed but "It's OK Deirdre, they're re-inflating it". My mum got straight back into her car as, unlike my dad, she knows how important lungs are. I was only semi-conscious at the time, but I remember the junior doctor rushing in and (probably) panicking a bit. With a blade, that I remember looking suspiciously like a Stanley knife, he cut a hole in the side of me, inserted a tube and inflated my lung. In my delirious image-obsessed and morphine-induced mind I was worried about the scar that would be left on my chest. He was saving my life and I was worried about the scar, notwithstanding the twenty-two inch sucker on my back. As a vain teenager I was clearly only bothered about what was visible. I still am.

Evidently, so is my dad. My old friend Mooney recently visited us from Canada where he had undergone major knee and leg surgery following a crash off his mountain bike in Whistler. Dad inspected it and said, "Wow, that's the biggest scar I've ever seen!". At that point Mum reminded him of the two-foot scar on his own son's back. He cares really, he's just a little forgetful at times.

The re-inflation worked. I was later transferred to an adult ward, which was horrendous, full of the nearly-dead and smelling of cabbage. After a few hours they transferred me to the kids' ward. I much preferred to be the old kid rather than the young adult on this occasion. Soon I became sure that I was doing fine and was well on my way to recovery. I called my friend Matt Pickering on the hospital phone. He wasn't in, so I spoke to his mum for a while. It was quite clear to me that I had given her a succinct run-through of how things were going and asked her to say hi to Matt. I learned later that the conversation was an incoherent stream of me blabbering on and totally ignoring her responses before hanging up on her.

I was on cloud nine at the time. Morphine cloud nine. In fact, I had been given a self-administering morphine drip, which allowed me to manage my pain relief by pushing a button when I felt I needed it. I'd boshed through twelve hours worth in two hours and was stoned out of my mind. As I came to, I realised I'd taken far too much and from then on was much more careful of when I hit the button. After I came off the drip I went onto oral doses and, instead, just asked for pain relief when I needed it.

It was good sheeet. Over the coming weeks I became thoroughly addicted to morphine. My days consisted of cycles of blissful morphine-nothingness followed by increasing awareness and pain. The drug withdrawal symptoms later proved to be very tough. The morphine took me to a 'Happy Gilmore' happy place. This included more than just the pain in my back, I mean *everything*. My concerns about being reliant on a wheelchair vanished, any constraints or concerns about the future went too. The pain was gone, hell 'the present' was gone! Whilst I've never been one to suffer a sensation of overbearing gloominess or depression, I remember the absence of all my challenges as being utterly blissful. Perhaps a glimpse of what a less challenged existence might be. Not necessarily the alleviation of something I couldn't cope with, but it was blissful nonetheless.

But don't take drugs.

They'll mess you up.

After a couple of weeks, I was able to sit in my wheelchair for short periods and I timed these with visits from friends. They would push me into the quad and I remember the pleasure of breathing fresh air and feeling the wind on my face. After about five minutes though, the pain in my back would become unbearable and I'd have to be put back to bed.

When I left hospital I weighed six stone (38kg, 84lb). The withdrawal symptoms from the morphine made eating difficult and sleeping was near impossible. For the first few months, my parents took turns to sleep in my room as I needed to be turned every two hours throughout the night.

And then my GCSE results arrived. I got two As, four Bs and

two Cs. I was gutted, my friends got all As. Jonny got eight A*s and two As, the twat. There were newspaper journalists talking to me and congratulating me, considering my circumstances. I didn't understand this. I just hadn't done enough. I decided it would be different when I did my A-levels. The first thing was to recover.

Before long, I was able to spend most of the day in my chair. But during this period I learned about the complications and challenges I faced beyond the process of my impressive scar healing. During my first meal at home, I did nothing more than lift a fork to my mouth. The pain was so great I threw it, screaming in agony. My mum describes it as the worst blood-curdling scream she's ever heard. As a nurse, she heard a few screams – not a super-cool start to a big extended-family meal. This prompted an immediate ambulance trip back to hospital. They sent two ambulance crews, so that they could lift me carefully as they feared one of the rods was broken. It turned out that the bent rod in my back had ripped the muscles in my shoulder. Awful, but in time things got easier.

On reflection, the surgery has been mostly positive, I'm glad I had it done and I'd do it again. *But* it was a bigger deal than I'd thought. Dark Times.

Something that I hadn't appreciated before writing this chapter was the extent to which my back operation involved my *entire* family. The disruption was much greater than I appreciated. Whilst I was in hospital, my grandparents looked after the family and our home in Mum's absence. This also allowed my dad to visit me and keep on top of his business. I also owe thanks to my sisters for letting me hog their mum for so long. Once home, the entire family revolved around my recovery. I distracted everyone from everything – what an image obsessed sixteen-year-old I was. I'm embarrassed that I hadn't appreciated this fully until writing this chapter.

Now, I'm going to relate all this to the theme of this chapter – Cause and Effect – and taking responsibility for everything.

It was no more my fault that I had to consider having the operation than it is my fault I have Friedreich's Ataxia. It was something I was presented with. From my perspective I could either let FA get me or do something about it.

I decided to have the operation. It was my responsibility to deal with it.

If I didn't have the operation, it would still be my responsibility to deal with it. I think I learnt a lesson here. We can let life's events drive us or we can drive life. For me, the best way to drive it is to try to take responsibility for everything. It helps me to avoid blaming other people. And if I do, it helps me to stop.

By saying to ourselves that everything is *our* responsibility then, regardless of the situation, we can do something about it. If we blame other things/people then we have an easy way out to not deal with challenges: "It's not my fault, it's not my responsibility." I prefer: "It's not my fault but it's *still* my responsibility."

After the Summer-of-Pain, I started A-levels. At first my back pain meant I could only do half-days, but I built my strength from there. By Christmas, I was fully back at school and, in addition, I started going to the gym with Jimmy. Well, we actually only went once as the first thing I tried to do was a chest fly and I promptly ripped my shoulder again. This set me back but we started again a few weeks later. At first, it was just about mobility. I'd try doing lat-pull-downs (pulling a long bar down) – I could do three with no weights attached at all – but each time my shoulder would go into spasm. By way of (proud) reference, I now do this exercise with 72lb attached as part of my thrice-weekly one-hour workouts.

During A-Levels, I was put on the committee to choose the new Head Boy and Head Girl. We were discussing different heads and deputies and, naturally, I just supported my mates. At one point, I was asked to leave so that the committee could discuss if *I* should be Deputy Head Boy. I didn't want to be. I didn't want to be looked at more and have to do morning assemblies. To get out of it I turned to my geography teacher and said, "Graham, let's be clear about this, I would only consider being Head Boy if Jonny was my deputy." I was crossed off the list. I may have bested him at Chess Club but this was his destiny and everyone knew it. Jonny got Head Boy, Tom Sessions was Deputy.

I think the above two points say something about 'Cause and Effect' and taking responsibility. Specifically, it's to do with the option we sometimes have of taking responsibility for *not* doing things. For the back operation, I chose to do it. Other people choose not to. Neither choice is wrong or right. As long as the person makes a purposeful decision one way or another, then they're taking responsibility for their situation. For my back operation, my choice made me much more able to cope with the shit that followed.

Regarding the Head Boy thing, it was more to do with the practicalities of avoiding being made more the centre of attention when I got plenty of that already. My goal is to be more normal, not less. The idea of being at the front of assembly each day really didn't suit my aims. I talk about this in Chapter 4. Besides, Jonny would have killed himself before being my deputy again.

The two years of A-levels were otherwise much like my GCSEs. The increased workload was a shock to the system, but I adapted and soon returned to the familiar pattern of good friends, hard work and lots of laughs. I enjoyed the subjects more and actually quite liked the exams as they gave me the opportunity to demonstrate how much work I put in. Sad I know.

After my last exam, I was shattered but my parents persuaded me to go out. The chosen rendezvous was the Slug and Lettuce pub in York, AKA the *Slag and Fetish*. We all got hammered. Tom, Alex, Olly, Matty and George. Matty hadn't even finished his A-levels yet, but this is Matty. Everyone came back to my house. Mum had been to her life-drawing class and had made a big sign and stuck it on my bedroom wall: 'SCHOOL'S OUT FOREVER'.

I remember she asked, "What do you think?"

I said, "It's great Mum!" Being blurry-eyed and pissed I followed with, "What does it say?!". A clear sign that sometimes I forget to look around – particularly when hammered.

The party wasn't nearly over. It was decided at one point that I would start dancing. This consisted of me standing up and friends throwing me between them. I could put enough weight through my legs to pivot about and be thrown between everyone. Not the wisest thing to do, but note how far the back-op recovery had progressed by now.

As we were still immune to proper hangovers, everyone got completely hammered. Olly was, and still is, the best of all my friends at getting extra plastered. Later on, I was sitting in my room with Jonny. Olly put his head through the window:

Olly: "Are you two talking about my mum?!"
Us: "NO!"
Olly: "Well she's got great tits!"

Olly denies ever saying this.

Eventually we fell unconscious. I woke at 7a.m. to hear the stereo on full volume playing Mystify by INXS on repeat. This kind of thing went on for the rest of the summer. I had lots of big parties. Alex Bradley more or less spent all summer at my house, with his suitcase in the boot of his car.

These are just some experiences really, but I think I took responsibility for making them happen, and my parents were very good at letting/encouraging me. Also, I had great friends throughout. I was always very lucky with those I met and I still know most of them.

After the Summer-of-Pleasure, I went to the University of York to do Politics. It was my first choice. In a way, it was a blessing for access to mates, as they were now becoming my Personal Assistants (PAs). They had no cash and I needed a hand, a pretty sweet deal for both sides, as we would be hanging out together anyway.

I don't think my friendships from Uni have been as strong as friendships from school, and fewer of them have lasted. Still, I met lots of great people.

When I first arrived at James College halls with Mum and Dad I was dumbstruck at how small my room was. We had a wardrobe crisis – these facilities were not suited to my extensive clothing collection. It could have spelled disaster. Luckily, I was also given the room next door for my PA. This was useful as it meant I had more wardrobe space. I assumed my PAs wouldn't mind me nicking their space as I had seen their clothes and decided they didn't deserve it.

During the day, I had some help from an 'educational support worker'. I recruited a good friend, Mark Bednarski. He worked with me at Bootham and stayed with me for my first year at Uni. In the evening, I had a team of people to help – all friends – different guys on different nights. George was the main man, though. He had the least to do at the time, but he was known to go 'AWOB' at times. This was when he wasn't in his room, but you could smell that he had been there recently. AWOB stands for 'Absent With Out Bath'. George was not my closest friend at school, but we became great friends during my time at university. Also, the legend that is Tom Sessions helped me out – he is a Jedi knight and can fly. Then there were other new friends including 'J boy J' AKA 'Jegan' who is and was the most laid back guy… ever. He oozes coolness.

This was the beginning of the 'Inner Circle', which has grown only slightly over the years. More on this at the end of the book.

It was also the initiation of the term 'bitching', which is the preferred expression amongst my friends when it comes to who is acting as my PA. In fact, I know when a PA has become a proper friend when they start referring to their own job as 'bitching' without batting an eyelid.

While I was studying Politics at York Uni, I met someone who was to have a profound influence on my life and my career: Dr Adrian Leftwich (1940-2013). I got to know him well enough to call him Adrian rather than Dr Leftwich. To this day I remember him saying, "For God's sake Fraser, call me Adrian!" – a big deal for me. Adrian was internationally recognised as a 'don' of the politics of third world development. I could go on and on about his excellent viewpoints and arguments, but my friends tell me it's boring, so I won't. In fact that's a lie, I'll tell you about his profound influence on me later.

Adrian was the leader for the 'Politics of Development' course. I remember having several relatively dry and boring lectures during my first term. Adrian's were different. It was the first lecture I particularly remember. A big auditorium, three hundred-plus students. He waited for everyone to sit down while walking up and down the stage carrying a pile of crappy OHP slides, which he then carefully put down. He stopped walking up and down, picked up the slides, blew the dust off them (a little dramatically, he'd obviously done it before), flopped them down again and said, "Right, let's begin." Immediate and total silence. He then began his lecture.

Not only did everyone pay attention, he also had them writing down exactly what he wanted. He had total rapport… it was amazing. I was still able to type at the time and Mark would also take notes, so I could cross reference later to ensure I'd got everything down. This allowed me to study Adrian's technique. I could see him recognise when everyone was just scribbling down and not actually listening. When this happened he'd break things up with an example. It would invariably be a story, such as, "When I worked in Geneva for the UN…" or a humorous story about "the weed known as Hashish". He was an excellent storyteller and orator. A master. I remember feeling wowed by this. I knew I couldn't be as good but I liked the idea of doing it anyway. I was watching a great speaker, and public speaking became one of my interests.

Throughout my studies at York, Adrian was consistently the lecturer I most enjoyed listening to and writing for. This was for a combination of reasons. Firstly, I greatly enjoyed the subject he covered, International Development. Secondly, I appreciated Adrian as an academic and as a person. He gave me the kind of feedback that taught me how to look objectively at problems. I could talk about this on an academic level for ages, but I will stick with the personal stuff as it's more interesting to most!

And this is relevant to Cause and Effect. Adrian helped me understand challenges and choices. Whether it was a lone man deciding to stand in front of a tank in Tiananmen square, or Nelson Mandela taking absolute responsibility for leading a new South Africa. Adrian helped me understand the absolute necessity of appreciating both sides of an argument. This comes before making statements of support or criticism to either side. Forming an opinion without appreciating both sides of an argument doesn't show an understanding of the situation.

Adrian also helped me understand how to take responsibility for any situation. He had a very interesting past in South Africa, it defined his and other peoples' futures. His story – which I'll tell you later – wasn't an easy one but I suspect it was on his mind when he gave me such bloody good advice.

This all happened long after I took responsibility for some of the challenges I have faced in my own life. But as I've explained, many of them were for silly reasons like vanity (obviously not that silly to me). Or maybe it was because I was forced to think in these ways earlier on in life. I think I made decisions at sixteen that most people don't have to make for years, if ever. With hindsight, I can see that I've taken responsibility for a lot of things. Because of Adrian, I'm able to do it far better.

Sadly, Adrian died in 2013. It's an event which has given me cause for regret for several reasons... not least the late writing of this book. Sorry Ado.

Before ending this chapter I'd like to return to skiing. Taking absolute responsibility is at the heart of that too. If I wasn't able to take responsibility for my situation, then I would not have the desire or will to go skiing. Why do I say this?

Well, I simply can't ski like an able-bodied person. If I failed to take responsibility for my circumstances, then I would say to myself, "Friedreich's Ataxia means I can't walk, therefore I can't ski." By taking responsibility for my situation I'm far more empowered to say, "I can't walk because of Friedreich's Ataxia, but it's still my *responsibility* to go ski!"

In his 'Enterprising Mindset' seminars, Jimmy often uses a video from my ski trips to explain this. Enterprising Mindset is a hobby business he created after completing his MBA and started a few businesses. He guest lectures and runs seminars on enterprise and entrepreneurship at universities, businesses and other organisations. In a section called 'How to Seek Opportunities', he makes three suggestions. A good place to start is by looking around you, followed by taking responsibility, and then embracing a perspective of resourcefulness. Jimmy feels my ski trips sum this up nicely. I suppose I do too, so I give him permission to use them as long as he only shows videos that make me look good.

Vanity really does rock.

Chapter 3

Resource vs. Resourcefulness.
Being resourceful in the face of resource
limitation.

Here we go again with a chapter title I would normally call 'a bit Wardo'. By this I mean it is the type of thing Jimmy would say and Wardo is his nickname in certain circles... specifically my inner circle.

But I like it.

In the first two chapters I talked about 'looking around you' and 'cause and effect'. These are vital as they give me the platform to 'do the doing'. This chapter is about the doing – the action after 'I've Decided'.

It's about focussing on what I *can* do, not what I *can't*. It would be very easy for me to say "I can't" a lot in my life.

Without the perspectives I have taken, I'd be right. This is not a unique way of looking at the world, unfortunately I'm not that clever. For me, *"How* can I do that?" is better than "I can't do that because".

I'll kick off with an example of abject failure by wheeling out a girl story... hold tight.

Let's go back to Seattle, when we did the road trip in the USA. It was a couple of days after receiving that topless lap dance from a Playboy model in a nightclub... and still managing to miss it.

Anyway, the trauma was short lived – I'm hard.

In that instance I was guilty of not 'looking around me' or, more specifically, 'not looking right in front of me'. A few days later, it was my outstandingly bad chat that was to blame for casting aside another pretty and well-meaning girl.

Let's re-join our North American RV road trip. After Seattle, we headed inland in search of national parks and epic scenery. And yes we did get a mild dose of cabin fever. Four lads in an RV for thirty days does strange things to your sanity. This can involve a new-found appreciation for Lionel Riche's 'All Night Long', particularly at full volume for thirty-second bursts in a campsite shower room or at the dead of night in a forest. Super cool, we know where it's at. Anyway – girl chat. We were in Glacier National Park, in Montana, and had been out drinking in a trendy rustic lodge where we met a cool and hot American girl. We had parked the RV nearby and, lo and behold, she suggested she walk back with us. Obviously she was impressed by my superior physique and outstanding chat.

The problem was that I really needed to go for a piss.

In my infinite wisdom, I decided to hold it in as long as humanly possible. It was a classic 'Inner Circle' moment. When we got to the RV, Rory and Tom went to sort out the inside to receive guests and make way for my wheelchair so that I could go pee. Meanwhile, Alex and I stayed outside chatting with the girl.

When the moment was right, Rory and I would go into the bus first and Tom would keep chatting to our new friend until I was ready. This is normal Inner Circle stuff. Everyone knew exactly what was going on without discussing it. My friends are at one with my bladder. A bit like how twins finish each other's sentences.

Anyway, the girl didn't know this. The problem was that my need for a piss had gone from serious to critical - it was a burning desire that I was struggling to control.

I kept making idle chat and answering her questions. My answers became shorter and shorter; I was keen to draw the conversation to an end. The loo was now my only priority. The questions kept coming, the answers became blunter, culminating with what follows. Although it pains me, I will give as accurate a transcript as possible... don't worry it's brief.

GIRL: "So Fraser, what do you think of American girls?"
ME: "Well, most Americans are fat and so are most of the women." Realising how rude this sounded, I followed with. "But not you, you're not *that* fat."

Cue, two-seconds of dead silence.

This was as Rory and Tom both drew breath before bursting into laughter inside the RV and dropping their beer bottles as they did so. The girl looked at me with a slowly shaking head as a mixture of hurt, pity and anger crossed her attractive face.

Well, it stopped her asking questions! When I returned, she'd decided to head back to her place for some reason. I expect she was tired.

I have bad girl chat, especially when desperate for a piss. It's a resource limitation of mine and I failed to think of a resourceful way around it. Yes, there were lots of 'could've, would've, should've' thoughts. *It will not happen again.* If the girl is reading this, I'm actually quite nice… honest.

Aside from learning that it is best to be honest when you need the loo, it's a good example of the need to be resourceful. I'll move on now to give an example of resourcefulness that's been really successful for me – skiing. I've explained that skiing only came into my life because I looked in the first place. Also, that my willingness to have a go was a function of taking responsibility for the position I'm in, despite it not being my fault.

So, that was 'finding' and 'being willing'.

Now we're talking about the 'doing'. The thing is, I can't stand and therefore I can't ski like most people. Maybe that could be excuse enough not to try. Except that it isn't, because statements beginning with "I can't do that because", are something I do not accept.

The "I can't because" statement will, by definition, always result in failure because hidden in the statement is the decision to do fuck all. So, to go skiing I had to ask, *"How* can I go skiing?" It turns out there's a whole world of ingenious engineers, commercial organisations and skilled teachers, who have asked the same question. These are the sit-ski manufacturers, ski resort operators and the employees and volunteers who run disabled ski programmes.

I'd like to make a short statement about this last paragraph. It's one that I don't think will sit well with some people, but it is true. I don't like 'disabled community' chat – at all. From time to time I have been introduced to other disabled people, particularly in Whistler. The reason is, that despite the circumstances I find myself in I don't feel I'm part of any community. I use the services available to me but I am not in any sort of club. I respect those who do similar things to the things I do, but we're not the same. An analogy in my mind would be assuming two black people will get along because they're black. That would be an outrageous statement. Or saying, "Oh you're gay, that's great, my friend is gay, you'll get along, as you're both homos."

This isn't logical thinking. However, I acknowledge this is also a problem *I* have. I can see that there are strong friendships and communities amongst disabled people. It's just a club I've chosen not to join.

OK, back to my 'how' story, where I skied in an area which is somewhat kinkily named 'Spanky's Ladder'.

It was a day with James, the slightly nutty risk-taking instructor who likes to push the limits a little further than most. The day was sunny after a fresh snowfall (tons of powder – sixty-two centimetres overnight!). He suggested we go 'over there' and I said "Yes." He was referring to Spanky's Ladder, which is a steep *uphill* section of the mountain that skiers climb in order to gain access to a large, challenging and less trampled ski area. The climb is tricky, made very difficult with so much snow and even harder by the fact that I was sitting down. This is a story of great importance to me. I will return to it later on but I want to talk about it now, as it has particular relevance to this chapter.

For your interest, and to mix things up a bit, I'm going to

tell this story by way of two letters that were printed in the 'Pique', Whistler's local newspaper, in quick succession over the following two weeks. It also has the benefit of giving Jimmy a quick six-hundred-and-twenty-six words without having to type them. The first is from a lady who saw what we did. The second is my reply, which I wrote with Jimmy on the flight back to the UK.

January 29th, 2010

The climb to the top of the ladder

As I sit and watch the snow falling on Monday morning I am reminded of my day on the hill two Saturdays ago. Anyone who was up on that 62cm day would have to agree that it was one of the best days we have had this season. There was more snow than my legs could handle and the mountains did a stellar job of getting everything open - kudos to WB [Whistler Blackcomb, the ski resort] for that.

But what made my day the most memorable was what my ski partner and hundreds of others climbing Spanky's Ladder saw that Saturday afternoon. It was the group in front of us slowly making their way up Spanky's for some freshies of their own. What made this group so remarkable was that everyone there was working extra hard to get up that damn ladder... because one guy was in a sit-ski. That's right, a sit-ski.

There were times when he was sideways, times when we thought he was going to start going back downhill and times when we thought everyone else behind him was going to go down too. But thanks to the efforts of everyone there, including anybody around who could help by carrying skis, poles, etc., the gang made it to the top safe and sound. Talk about getting a group pumped up - there were cheers galore as the whole crowd got carried away in the spirit of what it means to get out there and play.

So I just wanted to say thanks to the guy in the sit-

ski and thanks to everyone who made it happen - you've truly inspired me. Maybe you guys do this all the time but it was a first for me to witness what will be one of the most memorable events I have seen on the mountains and here in Whistler.

Cindy Bonnell

Whistler

And here was my reply...

February 5th, 2010

Climbing the ladder sitting down...

My name is Fraser Kennedy, the sit-skier who went up Spanky's Ladder a few weeks ago. I'd like to thank Cindy for her kind and uplifting words in the letter she sent the Pique (29th January).

But as I read and re-read her letter I felt a strong need to clarify a few points on what actually happened that day. The idea of climbing the ladder was not mine but my instructors, I just said 'yes'. The climb to the top was only made possible by the Whistler Adaptive Sports Team, a few good friends, and a good deal more strangers who carried their gear. It was a piece of cake for me!

Make no mistake, my ski down was unbelievable! But then so is EVERY day in Whistler. And it's not just the skiing; the goodwill and kindness towards guys like me is magnificent in Whistler – including you Cindy with your kind words.

So, it gets me thinking, who's the source of inspiration

here? Without the huge amount of goodwill, kindness and gritty determination of those involved in the Whistler Adaptive Sports Program (WASP) and the warm appreciation that floods from the wider Whistler community, I simply wouldn't have had the opportunity or willpower to say "yes". Without all of these people, you people, that day on Spanky's simply wouldn't have happened.

So thanks to you all, but especially you Gil, James, Glen, Sherree, John and all the WASP volunteers, every last one of you. Is there one piece of advice I could give? Easy, say "yes" more everybody, see what unfolds in front of you.

Fraz

PS - Cindy I'm coming back in March, come ski with us, I never get bored of skipping the lift lines!!

This is 'How Central'.

James, the instructor, took the absolutely impossible and figured out how to do it. What is interesting is that people generally gravitate towards this sort of thing and are more than willing to help out. James and Glen, my other instructor that day, along with Jimmy and Alex, asked those passing to take a pole or a ski for them so that they could help with pushing the sit-ski (and me) up. Everyone was happy to help – people like 'how' thinking. They even write in to newspapers when they see it.

The fallout from Spanky's Ladder was quite big. James got a *major* bollocking as it broke a few rules – I think it broke all of them. In fact, WASP wrote a new rule banning sit-skis from Spanky's after we did it. Before that, they didn't realise they needed one! Gil, my all time number one ski instructor, still grinds his teeth when he hears mention of it and particularly how "That really PISSSSESS ME OFF!" – this is Gil's trademark expression (Gil, I've given you one of these books, therefore you are reading this bit, so I'm sorry to bring it up again). But it does illustrate *how* to take on challenges – *by being resourceful in the face of resource limitation.* The obvious resource limitation was my inability to walk up that slope. The resourcefulness was James's quick thinking and ballsy outlook. Once the spark was generated then, a whole sequence of events followed, leaving me on the top of the mountain and Cindy sitting in front of her computer writing that letter. My only contribution was to say 'yes', when I had the option to say 'no'. I concede that this was a contribution, but in my opinion, it could hardly have been a smaller one.

One of the qualities I have is an inability to accept things and so, I find it quite easy to first seek alternatives by using 'how' thinking. It's an effective way of circumventing reality. It actually changes my reality. To me, acceptance is rarely 'winning' or 'coping'. More often than not it's 'giving up'. I think I do this to a fault at times, as this clashes with some of my real limitations. But I believe a 'no limitations' attitude is a better philosophy than the alternative.

I'll try and illustrate why I find this helpful.

I'd like to talk about what I call 'Dark Times'. These are the times we all get when we're overwhelmed by events and it hits us in deep and painful ways. Lisa, our editor in chief, was asking me about this and whether I would be willing to talk more about it in the book. I found it hard to answer her. After much reflection, I realised why. I just don't have these episodes nearly as much as people might imagine.

The Dark Times I can think of include Adrian dying. But I know that with the passage of time, we all lose people who are close to us.

Also, I find the nitty-gritty of being disabled quite depressing. At the time of writing I'm in the middle of a major 'assistance review', which examines what help I have, what has changed and therefore what additional help I'll need in the coming months and years before the next review. It sucks hairy balls. It reminds me how reliant I am on others; the whole getting up and getting dressed routines, eating, getting about, using my oxygen concentrator at night – the whole shebang. Spending time looking at these things is stressful and tiring. It's upsetting and, as much as I detest it, I can't change it so, I must *accept* it and move on. My mum taught me a lot here; the importance of being tough at times. I could learn more of course.

My back surgery was also bad - the pain, hospital, drugs, and recovery.

More pervasively, the Dark Times creep in when I'm reminded that my sight and hearing are getting worse and my voice is getting more slurred. Things I used to have no problem with – reading the paper, typing, speaking on the phone. The way I've fixed this is to remain very focused. I keep focused on what I'm doing next, to keep going, always taking steps, making plans, setting challenges. This way there is no need to dwell on what's happening to me. This is a skill I've learnt from Dad, the ability to move on, to fight and to wrest control.

I hope you can see that whether I can do something or not about the above examples, determines how well I'm able to cope with them. Adrian dying and my care reviews are things over which I have little control. I understand this but, nonetheless, they suck because I can do little else but accept them and move on. Perhaps surprisingly, I *can* do something about my failing senses; namely plan adventures. The difference here is that my speech and hearing are my problems alone and so I can fight them. I can chose not to accept them and then actively prove it by doing something straight away.

So, while I can talk about them, I don't actually have as many really dark days as you might expect. Normally, my dark feelings last maybe twenty minutes and then I try and kick my own ass out of it. And there are *always* things to focus on once you get used to looking around you and taking responsibility. For example, when I plan a Whistler trip, I immediately have *multiple* foci – strength and flexibility training, diet, sorting flights and carers, organising who's going to be where and when, working on my wardrobe choices (!). All of these are tiny little steps, and all of these steps keep me focused on where I want to be.

Talking about resource limitations versus resourcefulness, I can't stress strongly enough how important this is to me.

Despite what I've said above, I suspect some people will still find it surprising that I don't have many dark days. After all, I'm big-time disabled. I believe this is a function of people projecting their view of me from their own perspective. Something I try to explain later, is how Adrian taught me that everything is context-specific. This emphatically includes me and the challenges I have to deal with. This comes back to my initial thoughts on why I wanted to write this book. We are writing a book that focuses on the 'how', the perspectives to take and the actions I make. This dance between taking responsibility, how thinking, tiny little steps and looking around me, are more or less what this book is about. It's what bridges the gap between 'stranded in my own bed every morning' and 'awesome life'.

As I've said, I rarely get depressed, angry or anxious. It does happen, but it's relatively rare. If people accept the hand that life has dealt them, then that's not very exciting, interesting or fulfilling. When I reflect (I don't much), lots/all of the key people in my life got to where they are by themselves. The way I see it they do 'not accepting' very well – they tend to be ambitious and resourceful.

My point is to ask you to remember not to accept what you're dealt. I don't mind what you're dealt, just don't accept it. Even if you're born into great health and wealth, if you just accept it you will run the risk of becoming a posh wanker (and depressed from what I've seen). If you're born into difficulty, then the answer is the same... screw it, fight your adversity.

Perhaps I push it too far at times. Like when I crashed in Whistler. It might be a result of what life required of me from an early age. Big early challenges required big action. I've benefited from a sort of 'altitude training' powered by Friedreich's Ataxia. I've plenty of examples of when I've pushed too far and I'm not going to pretend I have nothing to learn. I'd be tempted to say this is just the way I am, but that is just slipping back to resource limitation. It is also what happens just before I get angry/depressed.

All right, now let's lift the mood and talk about how getting pissed at university, combined with contracting another rubbish illness, helped me become fitter, stronger and happier.

After my first year at university (and the associated wardrobe crises in student accommodation), I moved into Albemarle

Road. This was a property that we turned from an old bakery into a bachelor pad par excellence. My dad invested some money in it and Rory invested even more sweat in it. Initially, I lived with two friends and we always had people to stay. I operated an open door policy for good-looking people but the main residents were the infamous Rory, my close friend and carer from Bootham School, and the seriously cool Jegan, my good and chilled out university friend.

If I list a few features, you will see why this place became one big party house:

1. One of the interesting side-effects of using a wheelchair is that you have a strong preference for:
   - Open plan living.
   - Hard flooring, with the added benefit of being impervious to spilt beer/wine/anything.
2. I had a hi-fi so loud that it made the patio doors rattle.
3. My mum has interior design flair, so the house was functional and very cool.
4. Our neighbour was deaf, not once did she complain. What a lovely lady.

Albemarle Road parties were big and well attended... good times!

That house and its parties also helped me establish my reputation at university and I enjoyed what came with it. Lots of friends, living in a place others gravitated to, and being the host of the biggest parties.

This isn't a bad example of being resourceful in the face of resource limitation. I'll explain.

My friends' places were often in old houses or upper-floor

flats. They weren't very easy for me to visit. Also, the pubs and clubs in York (a medieval city) were often in old buildings with limited accessibility. We always found a way to go wherever we wanted, but having Albemarle Road as the 'base' for lots of parties was a huge advantage. So, I'm not joking when I say its specification helped me socially. Thanks Mum and Dad.

Over the years, Albemarle Road also played host to returning old friends. As they left university, a steady stream came to stay and rent a room. It was like a landing pad for others' circumstances and/or financial adversity! This included Matty, George, Mark, Ian, Eleri, Liz, Ol, Ben, Sarah, Alex's brother Damian, co-author Jimmy and, from time to time, just about everyone I've known.

Party-wise, we began to 'own' Christmas with a regular slot between Christmas and New Year's Eve. Jimmy and George developed a liking for themed parties – Après Ski, Zoolander, Gangster and others. We did this so that we could get the girls to look hot. George would make huge volumes of high quality cocktails. This was to get these hot girls drunk. It worked. Tom and Jonny both married their hot girls, Kate and Claire. 'Albelove' had arrived. University was proving fun and my accommodation was helping me.

Now I'll describe how a *new* rubbish illness came along, and how it *helped* me. As well as enjoying life, I was at university so had to go to class!

I liked all my university lectures. Just to remind you, I studied Politics at York University (yes, I am really interesting... it's true, my mum tells me so). During my second year I decided to go down the international route. I enjoyed these modules more and had lots of lectures with Adrian Leftwich.

The work pressure built up at this point. The exams were exhausting for me and my PA Rory, and even more so because

I had to have 50% extra time to allow for my slow typing. The week after my final exams I had two five-thousand word essays to submit. Unfortunately for Rory, this resulted in 4a.m. starts and bed at 9p.m. (I still can't understand why he complained). For the final essay, I was working until 11p.m., got up again at 3a.m., finished and submitted the essay at 11a.m. (the deadline).

Rory was not overjoyed. Neither was I. I was knackered.

The one 'first' (top grade) I got in my degree was on one of Adrian's courses in Developmental State Theory. For those of you who care, it was to do with socio-economic development in Vietnam, for which I did lots of research. This included driving to the British Library at Boston Spa, which was a thirty-minute journey and required security checks to get in. I felt like a secret agent. Bearing in mind that I was still an undergraduate, you could describe me as 'a bit keen' at times.

It was on the back of this that things went wrong.

During the summer, between year two and three, I had another essay to do. It was interesting and I figured I'd throw myself into it like I had done with that 'first' scoring essay the term before. I knew what I needed to do. But instead, I began to stumble and got very tired very quickly. I frequently got muddled and confused with the basics of it all. At the time, I was going to the gym a lot with Jimmy. We both noticed I was getting knackered. We were quite into 'gymming' by now so, like a proper athlete, Jimmy suggested 'Powerade' to give me a sugar and electrolyte hit. I'd drink it and it sort of worked but then I'd be knackered and bursting for a piss.

I stumbled through the essay and got a 2:2 (like a grade 'c'). This was disastrous, because I thought my essay was brilliant and the markers had failed to understand. They obviously hadn't. The final straw came when I went to the pub for lunch with Mum and Dad and had to come home before we'd even ordered because I felt so bad.

Mum, ever the nurse, tested my urine (yes, we have lots of weird strips in the house). Luckily, I wasn't pregnant. But my urine did have a lot of sugar in it. Mum explained that this meant I was diabetic and called the GP. The doctor tested my blood, she couldn't tell us how high my blood sugar was, as it was higher than her machine would read – I was massively hyper-glycaemic. I was sent straight to hospital and put on an insulin drip. I remember the doctor coming round and explaining that I was officially Type 1 diabetic.

With hindsight, Jimmy's Powerade suggestion, with its elaborate combination of fast-acting sugars, wasn't the best recommendation I've ever had.

This, as it turns out, is a common complication with Friedreich's Ataxia, I just didn't get the memo. It means I will always have to take at least five injections a day to control my blood sugar levels. My diabetes doctor explained that, over time, there was a 90% chance I'd need to take more insulin.

This wasn't the best twenty-first birthday present ever... but it turned out to be a blessing in disguise.

I decided that I'd challenge the odds. I wanted to minimise the diabetic effects on my health. Reading up on it, this meant watching what I ate to minimise how much sugar I put in my body, not getting too hungry, and avoiding getting fat. Exercising regularly also makes a big difference, so I stepped it up in the gym and became more focussed than ever before. And what a journey the gym has been. I'd like to share it with you.

While Jimmy and I had been going to the gym about once a

week for several years, when I was twenty-one it really jumped up a gear. Diabetes was a big factor, but there were other reasons too. It was proving to be a difficult year for me. Jimmy and his girlfriend went travelling in January, university work was full on and all my school friends were at Uni.

I came to a realisation. I was a bit 'ronery'... poor little Fraz.

So, I decided to make it into a positive. I *threw* myself into my dissertation and the gym. Jimmy was always doing heavier weights than me, I knew what he was lifting so, my target should be obvious to you already. The week he left I booked in ten sessions with a personal trainer, 'David', at a local gym. I liked it so much I quickly ramped up to three sessions a week.

I was at Albemarle Road the day Jimmy got back; he strolled in all tanned and excited. We talked about his last few months of adventures. After about thirty minutes we decided to go for a drink at the pub, conveniently opposite the house. I took my cardigan off. Jimmy took one look at my arms and shouted "What the hell is that? You've got man arms!", before inspecting and prodding me. I hadn't thought about the effect my cardigan removal would have, honest. It was very funny and gratifying. I'd not mentioned my fitness goals to Jimmy and I had really piled on the muscle weight. His tan may have been deep and his stories exciting, but I destroyed him when we went back to gym – it was joyful.

I continued going regularly to the gym. After about two years I started two-timing David with another trainer. This is a man for whom I have huge admiration, the 'Beefcake' Mark Basset. He's been my trainer for ten years now and his ability to think in 'how' terms is awesome. The gym and me are not natural friends. They represent able-body central. It's all about being able-bodied and becoming more so. So, the 'how' game gets turned up a notch when people like me arrive. Jimmy and I used to just do basic vanity stuff – arms, shoulders, back etc. He would 'spot me' on exercises and we figured out ways of using all sorts of equipment. David shifted it up a gear and got me my man arms. Mark has taken it to a whole new level. There is no exercise that Mark and I can't do. Core strength stuff, aerobic stuff, boxing, planks, free weights, quads, rear delts (I even know the lingo), lateral pull-down, pull-ups and lots more. Mark is a professional, a good mate and, helpfully, built like a brick shit-house.

If everything has gone to plan there will be a shot or two of us in the gym in the picture section of this book. What a 'how' journey it's been.

Having diabetes has in fact made me more aware of what I eat and how much I drink. Neither was bad or out of control at all. But the new circumstances meant a new approach.

I'm far stronger now than I would've been if I didn't have diabetes. And, as you know already, 'vanity rocks', so it helped my self-image. In addition, it gave me focus and discipline. Relating diabetes to my back op; it was a big risk that involved years of recovery and compromise. But I hadn't yet benefited from the operation's promise of a better/fitter life. Diabetes kick-started that process. The need to get fit took me from 'basically recovered' to 'fully improving my life'.

It gets better. The gym isn't a chore for me, I enjoy it hugely. It's helped me make new friends, like Mark, and manage stress by giving me a periodic physical and mental blow out.

The results?
- I'm now on less insulin than I needed when I was diagnosed fourteen years ago.
- My blood tests are very good on other measures.
- To quote my diabetes doctor: "Your blood is so well controlled, you are within the top 5% of people without diabetes. The fact you've done that is a huge achievement, I have no other patients that are so well controlled."
- I was able to re-engage with academia and work.

Of course, I'm proud of this achievement, but I also think it's representative of what we've discussed thus far in the book.

Specifically:
- Looking around me: There are a lot of physical things I can't do; it was my job to look for what I could do; it would be very easy not to.
- Cause and Effect: It was not my fault I got diabetes, but it was my responsibility to manage it.
- Resource vs. Resourcefulness: It gave me the focus and urgency to look for the how.

By now, it will be apparent that I rely heavily on the assistance of others to make things happen in my life. For now though, we think it's time for the subject of fear and failure; the nitty-gritty of fucking-up, not wanting to fuck-up, and getting over fuck-ups.

Mum's not going to like that last sentence.

Chapter 4

Confidence and Control, Fear and Failure

This is going to be an interesting chapter for Jimmy and me. Up to now, the process of note-taking, reflection and writing has been a smoothish one. The process of matching my stories and experiences to the thematic structure we decided on was, on the whole, pretty straightforward. But now it changes... the fact is that we may not quite see eye-to-eye on this chapter.

Neither of us is saying this difference of perspective and opinion is good or bad. We both acknowledge it's there though, and in the course of writing this chapter it has narrowed considerably. We feel it's important to give you a heads up now, as it's going to play out a little differently. Perhaps this chapter is more descriptive of me rather than my, much preferred, 'how' chat. I therefore invite you to judge me. But in doing so, I hope you will understand things from my perspective.

In order to get there, we need to go to 'full disclosure'. So screw it, here we go. As you know the best way to get there is...

GIRL CHAT. In fact, all the girl chat so far has been leading up to this chapter, as I am shit at it.

(Grandma, it might be best if you skip the next few pages.)

Among all the issues that Friedreich's Ataxia requires you to deal with, one of them *isn't* bad girl chat.

As I tell Jimmy, the problem is that "I have no game". Various 'things' have happened with girls over the years. Snogs here, snuggles there, squeezes all over the place and the occasional "What the fuck?!" semi-relationship. Lets just say it's a story of pretty standard less-than-exemplary stuff. The problem, as I see it, is that I don't have sufficient self-confidence in this area of life, yet. It's to do with a limitation I have relating to a mixture of confidence and control.

You will have noticed that confidence and control relate to most things in my life. Having the 'confidence' to look for and take 'control' of events and opportunities. This interplay between confidence and control and how one links to the other, mostly works for me. I yearn for both in some way or another.

It works right up to the point where it doesn't! It's here that I've sometimes stumbled.

Like most people, I am a mix of my mum and dad.

Dad is a fixer in business and in life – he welcomes challenges and fixes them. When there are problems he fixes them. When things are fine he tries to improve them. He is the same in business, always fixing broken things and trying to improve. At times I feel sorry for his employees, because they don't necessarily have Mum's black belt savvyness to contain him. Those that do, tend to work with him for years. His ability to adapt, solve or react to problems with 'fixes' has been a big lesson for me in taking on challenges. A lot of fixing... It's the situations where he can't 'just fix it' that he stumbles.

Mum, on the other hand, is more comfortable with accepting problems and finding ways of dealing with them. Understanding, coping, absorbing, adapting. Also, she was a nurse before becoming a mega-mum, which must have given her huge experience on the 'un-fixability' of some challenges in life. Over the years, she has proved more able at helping Rebecca and me adapt and cope with what's going on.

Surprisingly, it's Mum who has the harder-nosed perspective at times. Specifically, where there is no escape. The 'it doesn't matter how much you want to fix it, this is happening and this is what we need to do'. She is actually much tougher than my dad in some ways.

In terms of their influence on me, Dad has instilled a 'fix it and don't compromise in the pursuit of excellence' attitude, which I've tried to use to positive effect. I like to think that I've tried to be like Mum too. I think I've succeeded, but perhaps not always as successfully at times.

Just as with other things in my life, the basic problem I have with girls is the complex interplay between confidence and control and accepting and not accepting.

I can see that being in a wheelchair means that things are different for me but, as I've said, I never ever accept that I'm disabled or in a 'community' of such people. Sure, I have Friedreich's Ataxia but, as I explained earlier, I don't assume I'm in some sort of club, so I don't accept or acknowledge my membership. I don't like it when others assume I'm in it either (It's condescending, so watch it!).

At the same time, I try to have high standards for everything. This includes things like wearing nice clothes, having salon-quality hair, being polite, showing appreciation and not flipping out when I, or someone around me, makes a mistake (Jimmy says I may not be the *best* at this last one!). It also extends to actively removing myself from people who are tossers. People have come and gone from my life over the years and, of course, many go away because of circumstances, but there is not a single person who stays in my life whom I don't hold in high esteem.

These statements might sound arrogant, but they are actually true for most areas in my life. Everyone's life is a jumble of compromise, mine included. But, in the areas I *can* control, things for which I have a 'fix it and don't compromise' attitude, I keep myself to high standards.

Girls fall into this equation. Especially, the standard I have set myself for their physical attractiveness. I fancy the ones that are super-friggin-hot. I know what a vain and shallow wanker looks like, and yes maybe I'm in this department. But I don't want to fail with girls and the standards I set myself are uncompromising, somewhat shallow and exceedingly vain. So much so that I've failed to find one.

I'll try to explain why here. Full disclosure central.

Let me first clarify what the vanity thing is all about. Firstly, yes it is indeed vanity. I acknowledge there's a certain futility to it all: taking excessive pride in and having insecurities about my appearance, caring very much about how others see me, and insisting on always keeping up my standards. But this stems from a desire to fit in, I'm conformity-driven at heart. This was the principle motivation to having my back operation when I was sixteen, to minimise my deviation from the norm. The gym is the same. Of course I will never be a 'gym weapon', but I sure as hell can do what I can about it (via 'how' thinking). In seeking conformity, my achievement has been to narrow the gap between where I'd otherwise be.

This is also why I like having nice clothes. I can be good at it. There are plenty of areas I can't be good at, but I focus on those I can. How I find these opportunities is something I've already talked about. But a desire to conform explains a lot about who I am.

Also, for girls. Whilst I'm clearly no expert, what I think I've learnt is that many romantic relationships are about compromise at the start – age, education, interests, location, physical attractiveness, money – it seems you rarely get it all. But when a relationship, or love even, grows, then these things become much less relevant. The strongest relationships I've seen are the ones where neither person takes any of the compromises for granted.

It occurs to me that it's this initial 'compromise' I have difficulty in getting over. I understand this point – I just have to look at any long-term relationship around me. With girls, however, I seek conformity, and the highest standard here is mega-babe. Therefore, I fancy hot ones, and fail.

I've got plenty of wonderful friendships with girls, maybe even more than most blokes. My challenge is to meet somebody I can build a different *kind* of relationship with. A relationship with depth – something sexier than a meaningful chat, yet more meaningful than a sloppy snog.

I reckon that I've probably met a few of these girls already. By this I mean girls who I would really like to spend time with and who want to spend time with me. A 'proper' girl. In truth, given my poor hearing and shitty eyesight (better known as 'crazy eyes'), there are probably plenty more I missed out on by not being aware of their existence in the first place.

This is heavy going; time to wheel out an example of girl-chat that is particularly embarrassing, even by my own standards…

It's a story of massive ironic irrelevance to 'Looking Around Me', but it sits well here for reasons that will become clear. I grappled with it for several days before deciding on disclosure, even to my close friends. And now, here, Jimmy is typing it out for general distribution.

As I've said, I'm pretty keen on going to the gym. When I go on holiday to Portugal (where we are writing this chapter, we writers do struggle, tough times!), I join a local gym, so I work out just as frequently as I do at home.

It was in Portugal, in 2012, that I started going to a new place and it was excellent. The right kit in the right environment, with lots of good-looking people, just what I like. As I was working out, I noticed a hot girl by the reception desk, who was also smiling at me, so I half smiled back without being a dick about it. As we left, I noticed her again but couldn't get a proper look, as I don't wear my glasses in the gym.

On the way back, I asked my PA, Garritt (G-dog), if he saw the hot girl. He hadn't noticed her, he prefers boys anyway so I figured he wasn't looking. And screw it, these things happen on holiday, what can you do? I just changed the conversation.

A couple of days later I was back in the gym and 'jackpot', she was there chatting and smiling with the lady at reception again. Obviously I dropped into super-cool mode and kept my head focused on doing the biggest and most impressive looking exercises I do in the gym i.e. chest and 'guns' (biceps). When I did get a chance to look, I was chuffed to see that she seemed to be looking over again.

As we finished up, I asked G-dog to pass me my prescription shades, which I'd taken off when we got in.

"I'll give them to you when we get outside," he replied.

"Now G-dog," I retorted.

With a slight huff, he got them out and put them on my head (he's good at the 'slight huff', it's in his nature). As we left I figured I'd just play it cool and if the girl and I caught each other's glance again, then I'd say hi. As we came to reception, jackpot, she looked over and we caught each other's eye. G-dog was pushing me at the time so I just gently squeezed one of the wheelchair wheels to turn the chair and take control – this is a normal 'hang on a minute' manoeuvre I do with my PAs. G-dog got the signal and stopped. I kept my gaze so as to fully focus on the girl, make sure I got her attention and then introduce myself.

As I did so, it became horribly clear that my charm wasn't going to result in friendship, blossoming romance or even a slap across the face. Alas, it would result in absolutely nothing. It turned out she was a cardboard cut-out advertising gym memberships!

Now I have a reputation for being a bit shallow at times, but this girl really was too shallow, even for me – two-dimension shallow.

I let go of the wheelchair wheel, G-dog asked me what was up and I said, "Nothing, lets go," as I bowed my head in shame. I think you'll understand why I wasn't particularly keen to share this epic failure. In fact, it played on my mind for a couple of days. What a ridiculous situation… a frigging cardboard cut out – the shame.

The blunt truth is that whilst I didn't have my glasses on, it's my 'crazy eyes' that were to blame. I *can* see but I just need longer to 'tune into' what's in front of me. The distance and busy-ness of the gym and weights, all added up to me getting it so massively wrong.

After a few days, I decided to mention it at the dinner table to the seven other friends I was on holiday with. Needless to say a lot of wine got spilt as they heard the punch line, which they *never* saw coming.

I hope it's become clear in this book that if there's one thing I think I've got 'down' in life, it's humility. If you find yourself in a position where you feel embarrassed, then a good start is to show humility. When you're clumsy like me you drop stuff and spill stuff. Rather than be anxious about the consequences, I find it's best to be humble about it. Humility beats embarrassment and humour puts everyone at ease.

In the next chapter, you'll find a huge point relating to this.

For me 'humility' = 'failure management'.

Humility is a public statement. You can't really show 'internal humility', you either show it or you don't. And, in my experience, it's an effective way of removing the baggage of self-image and endearing oneself to others. People appreciate honest people, who talk about the things they're scared of or embarrassed about.

So, was the cardboard cut-out chick a 'Looking Around Me' failure? Absolutely. Was it also a good example of overcoming a failure through humility? I hope you think so.

In fact, humility is very useful for overcoming most of my mistakes, screw-up and failures – I use it daily. There are lots of other ways of dealing with mistakes, of course, but the point is that failure is familiar to everyone and it's our responsibility to deal with it. This is especially so for the more serious matters in life.

As we'll see, guilt and responsibility are connected, but for now let's move on to fear.

In his enterprise seminars, Jimmy sometimes says that fear isn't actually *real*. I used to call it 'Jimmy Jabba'. As will become clear, I don't need or use this expression in my head, but it's worth covering here for those unfamiliar with the concept. It has helped Jimmy and me to understand what I now realise is a personality quirk of mine. Not necessarily a good quality, but there all the same.

As Jimmy describes it... when you're dealing with the feeling of 'fear', it doesn't hurt to first think about *at what point* fear appears. Fear is real in the sense that it's a documented emotion, and there is a useful ploy to help you deal with it. The point is that you never 'fear' anything that is in the past. The feeling of fear is always in the future, "I'm worried x will happen next week." or "What if y happens?"

It's impossible to fear a broken leg. When it actually happens you feel pain, it's happened. You feel the fear of the *possibility* of breaking your leg. And fear experienced once your leg is broken, will always *still* be in the future, "Will I be able to ride my bike again?" So, it's anxiety relating to something that hasn't happened yet. In a sense, it's not actually *real*, it's anticipation, and therefore it never actually happens like other sensations, such as pain or hunger.

In terms of managing fear, Jimmy's point would be that, if it isn't real then it's up to you how you handle it. And if you can handle it then, in time, you can realise that what you actually do and how well you do it is up to you. And fear, more often than not, holds people back irrationally. More importantly, it is something entirely within your control if you choose. After all, in a sense it's not actually real.

Jimmy then goes on to explain that what we set out to do in life is, by and large, our responsibility. Our ability to handle fear and anxiety plays a big part in what we choose to do. More often than not, it stops us doing things that we would otherwise really like to do. Objectively speaking, there's nothing stopping us other than our finding the will to do it. Therefore, the opinions you hold and the outcomes that follow are a function of your expectation. And misplaced or unchecked fear can warp your expectation hugely.

With this in mind, and the challenge of combining an interesting and fulfilling life with being disabled, it would be really easy to fear everything and avoid failure by doing nothing... and becoming depressed, frustrated and angry. I do feel these emotions sometimes. I get frustrated and angry more often than I'd like. Nonetheless, I try not to let them consume me.

When talking about things like paragliding and skiing, people often say, "You're really brave to do that Fraser." I don't like these statements because, from my perspective, there is nothing particularly admirable or brave about them. I just love going skiing and paragliding, like every other skier or paraglider. Hidden in these compliments is the implication that my being in a wheelchair makes me more 'brave'. It's just not the case.

On top of this, perhaps understandable, misconception, I don't believe I actually feel *personal* fear. Think of Jimmy's fear thing above as a way of understanding how I feel personal fear. In short, I don't much. I don't need to overcome it, as Jimmy describes. I'm not saying this is necessarily a good thing, in fact apparently it's a bit weird. Once I come to terms with any situation I find it relatively straightforward to accept the new reality and punch on through. This way isn't a bold or macho statement, maybe it's a fault. The best description I can give is that I'm wired that way.

Now I'd like to spend some time on bravery, because it's rather important.

There are two levels to the bravery-related statements in the two paragraphs above. The first one is a simple statement of fact, that when I ski or paraglide or take off on my world travels, I lay no more claim to bravery than others who do these things. Am I brave compared to those who are very fearful? OK maybe, but no more brave than the millions of others who travel and do exciting things like skiing. This is because, when I ski, I'm just a customer of a service that caters to the ability of its customers. The adaptive ski school focuses on those with limited mobility and/or cognition. They tailor their service to the requirements of their clients. In my case, a sit-ski. They're trained, experienced and insured like any other ski school. I get no bravery medals here and don't want any. The *second* point above warrants more discussion, as I *have* grappled with *other* aspects of bravery.

Looking up dictionary definitions, Jimmy and I found that bravery is described in several ways, which support the points I'm about to make. Here are a few paraphrased and unreferenced examples of the kind of things we found:

Bravery is:
- one's ability to endure or face unpleasantness or behaviour without showing fear.
- a quality of spirit that enables you to face danger or pain without showing fear.
- the quality that allows someone to do things that are dangerous or frightening: the quality or state of being brave.

Volition is kept curiously ambiguous here. The first two definitions say that if you can get through something without feeling fear then you are brave. The third talks about a *quality* that *allows* someone to do things that are dangerous or frightening.

Firstly, I think all three validate my point that the adventures I take are *not* acts of bravery. They're not any more frightening, unpleasant, dangerous, or painful for me than they are for anyone else. If you think so, then you're really not seeing it from my point of view. I would ask those who disagree with me here, to reconsider, as it's wrong, and it's more than a little exasperating when I hear it.

I do concede, however, that living with FA has been/is:

- Unpleasant – the condition's effects are a definition of unpleasant.
- Painful – back operation, physiotherapy, and various injuries.
- Dangerous – my physical fragility and general vulnerability means danger is always nearby.
- Frightening – the future's hardly rosy.

These are matter-of-fact statements, and the truth is I don't feel fear for myself. So, this says I'm very brave, right? I'm not so sure. It's the third definition we've looked at which brings to mind that it's an *action* that one chooses to undertake, devoid of fear, that defines bravery. Some soldiers claim only fools aren't afraid of battle and that only those who overcome this fear and act are brave. So, in this case I'm not brave, I'm nuts, I'm a crazy fool!

Despite this, I have not taken action, FA has acted upon me. *It is happening whether I like it or not.* In our discussions, Jimmy likened this to the bravery of a soldier being ordered over the top of a hill to take on the enemy. Regardless of whether he feels fear or not, if he runs over that hill and starts shooting, then that would define a brave act. I imagine I'd struggle to find anyone who disagrees with that statement. Suppose he's strapped to a trolley and is being *dragged* up that hill, gun in hand. And suppose he doesn't want to go over, if he had the option he wouldn't, and he would give almost anything not to, he'd sooner run away. Yet, over he goes, and he has no choice but to fire his gun. The only option he has is to turn the gun on himself before he gets to the top or just wait to be blown away by the enemy.

When you think about it, I'm the guy on the trolley. I don't want FA, I don't want to face the above nasties, but I have no choice. I am unconvinced that whether I am fearful or not determines my 'bravery', as it seriously undermines the efforts of the countless other people in my position, and worse, who *are* fearful but still do what's necessary (*necessary and unavoidable*). Are they not brave too?

Following this logic suggests that everyone born with a serious disorder automatically gains massive 'bravery' status that needs to be celebrated and revered. Taking this to absolute extremes, does it mean that those who do the unthinkable and kill themselves are dishonourable wimps? I don't believe that's joined up thinking and I think explains why I have legitimate claim that this issue is less clear than most people think.

When Jimmy and I started this section, my contention was that I'm not brave and it's a well-meaning misunderstanding when others think I am. After hearing me out, Jimmy agreed with me. Then, in the course of our discussions he reverted to the bravery thing. Then, having discussed it further we produced the above paragraph. I'll concede I've shown bravery at times and, without wishing to be a cock about it, I suppose I'm proud of that.

So, from my perspective, I don't really buy the 'disabled people are brave' thing. I imagine that this is the position taken by all sorts of people in difficult situations. For those who feel they are brave because they are disabled and coping with it, more power to them. As I said before, my opinion is but my own.

With all this in mind, I hope you can begin to understand why I now think that, perhaps, I don't have *enough* fear. The skiing accident I described in the first chapter is one example. It could have really messed me up and given other people lots of problems. I didn't feel any fear, but Jimmy felt it in relation to telling Mum and Dad that something horrible had happened. Then there's the 'Spanky's Ladder' story – one of the coolest experiences of my life. Whilst we would never have got permission to do it officially, nobody's convinced we did it as safely as we could. A bad crash there would have caused a huge number of problems for all sorts of people, not least myself. A bit more caution would likely have been good for everyone's sake, but not to do it would've been unthinkable (sorry Gil).

The fact that we boasted about it and took pictures, rather than just keeping it to ourselves, said much about our bullish pride. In fact, we had all agreed that we wouldn't make a big deal about it, but this went out the window when James used our Spanky's adventure as an excuse to his manager for being late down the mountain (wtf!?); and then Cindy wrote that letter to the newspaper!

It's the same with paragliding. On my big crash (where I missed the cows, hit a couple of hedges, crossed a field, went through a bramble bush, hit a tree, crossed a stream and a hit a stone wall), I honestly wasn't so worried about myself. It just doesn't kick in with me like it should. The whole 'life flashing before my eyes' thing, I only get that *after* the event and on a much more rational level. What I *do* get after the event is fear for others, I get that all the time. When I get close to pushing things too far, I should see the wider implications than just those for me; I know I should feel more fear. I like the analogy that if you're too fearful it sits in front of you and stops you doing what you really want to do. *I* feel that fear sits *behind* me too much. It would be better if it sat *next* to me to better qualify my actions.

How my missing out on *personal* fear came about is, perhaps, a function of my life to date. I imagine I'm like many people who've dealt with scary stuff in their early years. Not just degenerative disabled people; people born into conflict, poverty, violence and many other problematic situations that are far, far worse than mine. I imagine there are lots of ways to go, but I think my attitude probably originated with my staring up at the stars at my friend Tom's house when I was fourteen – the moment I realised things were going to be different for me.

Heavy, let's keep going with another disclosure on failure.

Earlier, I talked about how my ridiculously high standards mean that I don't meet girls much and miss opportunities. Take the cardboard girl story as an example: I was not 'looking around me' very well and my 'how' thinking was less than stellar! While it's a story that didn't involve anyone real (in a literal sense), and a heavy dose of humility and candour made it amusing, you'll notice it's another story about not meeting anyone.

The thing is this, I lack confidence with girls because there is something I can't accept about myself. How am I to get other people to accept something is wrong with me if *I* haven't come to terms with it myself?

Instead, I've built this coping mechanism that allows me to deal with things. If I know what I can't have and go for that, then I don't have to deal with anything else. I can still be me, hang out with friends, talk about girls and generally get on with life. I have come to realise that the fact that I've not met someone is a situation of my own causing. In a way, I've protected myself from the problem, because I've not been able to deal with it.

Whatever I call it or however I describe it, it's a failure that, on balance, I'm comfortable with. Whether this will remain true is something that is my responsibility to keep in mind. But for now it works for me. It's a case of controlling rather than compromising.

Talk about full disclosure (errr thanks Jim!). So, if you are really hot and single please get in touch. But as you will have gathered I'd really prefer a picture message to start... And people have the audacity to call me shallow.

In other areas of my life, my combination of accepting and not accepting often works very well for me. A recent example was a conversation I had with a specialist over an issue with my back. It's straight because of the rods I have in it. What has happened, however, is that my pelvis has begun to rotate below the rods. This meant that I wasn't sitting straight in the chair and one of my shoulders was becoming more raised. Clearly unacceptable - cue my 'fix-it' mentality!

I wanted to look at surgery options to get it fixed. We met a specialist and he wasn't keen to do the operation. In fact nobody around me thought I should even consider it. They were oblivious to the fact that vanity still rocks.

It was during the consultation that the doctor completely pissed me off and, I feel, demonstrates clearly my approach to dealing with problems. Over the course of the consultation he explained several scenarios, each of which had major compromises. The best option meant that my back would become straight but my legs would have to be strapped down – one problem leading to another. It became clear to me that surgery wasn't really the solution.

The surgeon then said the following, which caused everything to go awry:

"I'm glad you agree that the operation isn't right for you, because in truth you're not fit enough for the operation anyway."

"I am fit enough."

"I'm sorry, you're not."

"Yes I am."

This was truly irrational of me. A consultant surgeon had just said that the operation was unsuitable (and I agreed with him), and then he told me I wasn't fit enough to have it anyway, because it would be mortally risky. While I agreed it wasn't the right way to go, I couldn't take him telling me I couldn't handle the op. It then got even more awkward.

He said: "There is one other solution Fraser."

"OK, fine, what's that then?" I replied.

"You can accept it. Accept that things are wrong and move on."

'Go fuck yourself.' (I thought this Grandma, I *thought it*).

With hindsight, both of his statements directly challenged how I do things. I don't accept things, I fix them (like Dad) and I will tackle everything that I'm faced with (like Mum). These statements, 'you can't handle it' and 'just accept it' were therefore offensive to me. I was looking at ways of straightening my back and had just received a serious blow. I might have been a little prickly, but I stand by how I feel on this. It's an example of the way people can unintentionally provoke me.

The solution we found here, was to modify my wheelchair

so that I sit straight. My rotated pelvis is my little secret (well not so secret now, I suppose). The point is that it's not about accepting *anything*. It's been about taking responsibility for everything. Looking for options, taking responsibility and figuring a 'how' solution. 'Just accept it' statements are destructive and defeatist.

***

There you have it, my most fully disclosed chapter yet. It was also the last of my girl chat stories. Phew! Only kidding, we have held a couple back. The next chapter isn't really about me anyway, so I'll be grateful for the break.

In fact, the next chapter is about someone who lived a *properly* extraordinary life. It's a life that I hope will be remembered for a long time to come. Not just because the person in question is now dead. It is because, if you're anything like me, it requires you to seriously challenge a couple of pretty big preconceptions about the human condition and the challenges we all face. Heavy, I know!

Chapter 5

Communication

I don't pretend the title of this chapter is new. Everyone knows that effective communication is key to work and relationships, and a breakdown in communication is often the root of problems in business, friendships, romance, politics etc.

However, it gives me an opportunity to talk about someone else rather than me! This person is Adrian (Ado) Leftwich, my lecturer and friend at university, who later became my boss in international political development research. He greatly influenced both me and many others. You'll see how his influence extends far beyond 'Communication', but this is the chapter where Adrian belongs.

Firstly, it's important to clarify how particularly reliant I am on communication. Being immobile means that my ability to communicate consistently and concisely is at the very heart of my existence. Combining this with the fact that I can't write, and type very slowly, three words per minute slow, means that the spoken word is the most important tool for me. If I tell you that the effects of FA mean my speech is somewhat slurred and I generally speak in short sentences (six or seven words per breath), what I choose to say and how I say it *really* matters.

It is in the area of communication that I feel I learnt a huge amount from Adrian.

In his lectures I was fascinated by his rapport with his audience. He consistently held the attention of two hundred-plus people with the choice and delivery of his words. I remember wanting to have that power. To interact, challenge, create a similar rapport and have a dialogue with so many with such elegance. I didn't put it like this at the time, I just wanted to be 'good at communicating like him'.

When I chose my dissertation on Tiananmen Square, Adrian was my supervisor – jackpot. So, I moved from being a member of his audience to having one-on-one meetings. Adrian was a masterful communicator here too, and he made me do most of the talking. He was very good at tapping in to what I was thinking and, all too frequently, where I was going wrong. He would ask me to think in objective terms and look at all sides of an argument, 'everything is context-specific'. He'd then offer perhaps two sentences of sage wisdom and send me on my way, a slightly more enlightened undergraduate. All this in twenty-five minutes. While this was hugely beneficial academically, it's also something I try to use in my daily life. I try to see all sides before I decide what makes sense and what is just big hairy balls. For practical purposes, I can usually rely on examples of bollocks coming from my friend Olly's mouth.

After my degree, attempting to emulate my dad in business, I tried a few different things. I was extremely successful in demonstrating that I'm not an entrepreneur! Whilst I got things done and enjoyed it (in parts) I never felt I had either the talent or the natural enthusiasm for business. My interest was in academia. Particularly building rapport, bouncing ideas and drawing fair conclusions that stand up to critical review. I did two things. Firstly, I applied to go back to university to do a Master's degree in Conflict Governance and Development. Secondly, I decided to get my hands dirty and see what I was studying first hand. I organised a trip with George, Alex and Annabel (all Bootham School friends), to South Africa, Namibia, Botswana, and Zimbabwe. For Annabel, it was a trip with three sweaty, farty boys; she must have felt so special. For me it was an opportunity to test my commitment to my studies, to understand the reality behind the academic books and journals.

Apart from being a fabulous trip, it broadened all of our minds considerably. For me it represented exposure to the reality of politics and development. For George and Alex, it represented learning the importance of effective planning. This was shown in their attempt to climb Table Mountain in Cape Town wearing t-shirts and flip-flops. They got lost, night fell and they had to sleep rough. But it was OK, because they ended up spooning for most of the night to keep warm. They've never really looked each other in the eye since. It became very clear to Annabel that girls are much more pleasant to be around, are prettier and smell nicer. She was very tolerant.

Only a few days into the trip, I knew I'd made the right decision. If I got the offer, I was going to take it. The next morning I got the email saying I'd been accepted. 'Back of the net.'

Back in England, once underway with the Master's, my meetings with Adrian continued. This was especially the case later on in the course, as my thesis was on South Africa, a country Adrian was more or less booted out of in the mid 1960's.

After I'd got my MA, Adrian hired me to work on the

Developmental Leadership Program (DLP, www.dlprog. org). The DLP is a research group set-up by Adrian, who was research director, and Steve Hogg from AusAID, who had overall control, with a focus on the policy implications of the DLP's research. These two had the idea and managed to generate sufficient funding to make the dream a reality. The DLP looks at the role of leadership in development. Specifically, what the world can do to encourage good leadership in poor and politically fragile countries to help them become richer and more stable.

I was a researcher and database manager. Adrian gave me a really interesting project (well I think it was interesting) to build a web-database into which researchers all over the world could enter profile facts about leaders. No such database existed, so I built one. The database asked whether these people were alive or dead, and who they were: military leaders, elected politicians, heads of state, autocrats, tribal leaders etc. This allowed us to assess the relative socio-economic success or failure to try to find common themes and patterns. The kind of things we mapped varied hugely; from where they went to school, to whether their career was in politics or the military or business etc. I know, boring to most, but exciting to me!

I was invited to speak at a conference that Adrian was running at the World Bank headquarters in Washington DC.

When I travel I normally *used* to ditch my PAs and take a mate with me instead – it was Jimmy in this case (Jimmy: 'a good gig!'). This has changed over the years as all of my PAs become close mates before too long. More of them in the last chapter.

While Adrian and Steve were the main men at the conference, and without doubt the most informed and smartest guys in the room, Adrian only presented twice and Steve not at all. Adrian's presentations were at the beginning, to set the scene and again at the end, to conclude and bring all the distinctive research projects together. The projects varied hugely: understanding the importance of education in Mauritius; the economic growth of Botswana; the response to the HIV-AIDs epidemic in South Africa and Uganda, and much much more. I hope you get a sense of how sharp Adrian's mind was. He 'led from the back'. Steve didn't speak at all as Adrian was the head of research and this was a research conference. There was no ego problem between these guys.

The trust they put in me, a twenty-five-year-old MA student, to present one of the project's core components, something that had cost thousands, is something that still amazes me. And it wasn't just me. My colleague, Heather Lyne de Ver, presented her project to the group too. In fact we had two presentations each. Both of us were in seriously unchartered territory. Adrian not only gave us the opportunity to speak, but somehow also the *confidence* to do it. He would often ask my PAs for their opinions, too. When he wasn't off sightseeing, Jimmy was invited to contribute to the conference. He recalls that despite not knowing the topic at all, even *he* felt confident to speak.

For those of you who have not been to the World Bank HQ, I'd like to share a couple of observations. Frankly, it's a pretty self-indulgent organisation considering it's there to help poor people. It also caters to the culinary preferences of people from all over the world. This made the canteen really interesting to visit. People of every size, race, style of dress and language were consuming every food type man has ever conceived. It was like the bar in Star Wars where Luke meets Hans Solo for the first time. The sushi was excellent.

The point about Adrian is that I think he was *genuinely* more interested in what *others* had to say. An example that stands out was a conference in London that I attended with Heather and other team members. Dylan was my PA that day. Adrian had the ability to recognise when someone had enough intelligence and perspective to contribute. He turned to Dylan, "Dylan, from the layman's perspective, what do you see here?" Dylan started to speak without jargon and made a meaningful contribution to the discussion. Adrian said, "Dylan, you're sat too far away, come into the discussion group."

Dylan is a Kiwi with an outlook on life that is very refreshing and epitomises free-thinking. He is very intelligent and a master at seeing patterns of ironic absurdity. 'Esoteric' is one of his favourite words. One observation he made after the London conference was that Adrian's team looked like an international development 'A-team' of sorts. Adrian was Hannibal Smith, I was the techie dude in the wheelchair, Heather was the beautiful heroine, Steve the Crocodile Dundee trusted number two, and a couple of other hilariously allocated roles. Dylan decided he was the 'wild card' character, which I wholeheartedly endorsed. His hair was three feet long at the time and he has a tattoo on his back, which he describes as 'The Beast from the Southeast' as it contains the body parts of seven different animals in one strange entity. You'll get the idea that he is not someone who struggles to think outside the box. He lives outside it.

Rather than ignore him, Adrian had everyone shuffle their chairs so Dylan could fully engage with the debate. He was quite the natural, but it was Adrian and Steve who gave him the opportunity to communicate.

In terms of my understanding communication, Adrian showed me that 'looking like you care' isn't as effective as actually caring about other people's views. As I speak in truncated sentences, this means that I spend a lot of time asking other people questions. By actually caring, I think I've attracted more friends in my life. It's also a useful way for me to keep my chin up. I really enjoy and value good conversations.

Moving on to the other aspect of my friendship and appreciation for Adrian...

As I've said, he sadly died in 2013, following a short battle with cancer. As Jimmy was researching this chapter, he came across a selection of articles and interviews with Adrian, as well as a host of obituaries from national newspapers.

He learnt about a period in Adrian's early twenties that was both extraordinarily challenging and defining for him. Through our friendship, I had known about this period for some time.

In the early 1960's, Adrian had the dubious honour of becoming South Africa's first white political prisoner. He was an extreme anti-apartheid activist. His organisation blew things – not people – up. Worse still, he got caught. Worst of all, he became a state witness. This meant that many of his colleagues went to prison. Being a state witness also meant that he could get out and avoid a probable death sentence. He was very well known.

On my South Africa research tour, a family friend asked who my thesis supervisor was. When I mentioned Adrian, he was taken aback and called to his wife, "Fraser knows The Leftwich!". Adrian was, and will always be, a critical player in apartheid South Africa's history.

I know, heavy shit.

The first reason I'm bringing this up is because, despite having one hell of a bad period in his twenties, the subsequent life Adrian created for himself made a great difference to the world. The second reason was an article Jimmy came across, which prompted him to stop everything and call a meeting with me.

The Article was entitled 'Adrian Leftwich, The Unforgiven' (Davis, 2013). It quotes Adrian and talks about the remarkable process he went through in order to come to terms with his past. This culminated in him producing a paper entitled *I Gave The Names* (Leftwich, 2002). This is a widely read and much appreciated piece and I urge you to read it. Adrian also tried to make contact with those he testified against and, in some cases, succeeded.

In his paper, he talks about a conversation he had with a friend in London, in the early 1980's. He explains... 'We had talked about the events of that year countless times before. But then Jill, a person I knew and trusted completely, suddenly said: "No. It was not okay at all. Whatever the pressures were, it was not okay to behave like that."' (quoted in Davis, 2013).

Adrian describes how this statement struck him profoundly. After a long period of reflection, and therapy, he learnt what he describes as being the single most important lesson in his life – *to take responsibility for his actions.*

Jimmy and I discussed the peculiar similarity here with my own outlook. As I explained in the chapter 'Cause and Effect', it's not my fault I've got FA, but it's still my *responsibility* to deal with it. It might partly explain why Adrian and I got on so well. His actions in 1964 had become a curse for him over the years, including nightmares and a reliance on sleeping pills. It was learning to take responsibility for past actions that helped Adrian come to terms with them. In his case, it *was* his fault, but it was also his duty to take responsibility for it.

Adrian 'got' me and I 'got' him, even though we never talked about it. Adrian's influence on me was pretty big. Actually, it was life-changing. Working for him was interesting and exciting. The lessons I learnt run far beyond ordinary communication.

The passage of time had given Adrian the opportunity to reflect and find a new direction. And yet, the actions of his youth followed him for the rest of his life. In many people's eyes, redemption eluded him. In my eyes, Adrian Leftwich not only entirely redeemed himself, he also became a good man.

I thought the break from the previous chapter would be refreshing. In fact, talking about Adrian has been very difficult. I'll return to talking about myself now, and the theme of this Chapter: 'Communication'.

Adrian taught me a lot about both the importance of communication and how to do it well. Being able to explain something coherently is something I understand well. It's also something I'm inherently challenged by. Despite everything Adrian taught me, the truth is, I still struggle due to my eyes and ears being a bit crap. So, I've developed new ways of communicating which I didn't even tell *him* about.

My crazy eyes mean I find it increasingly difficult to see who I'm speaking to, cardboard or real. Also, my hearing is affected by background noise more than other people. I can hear fine but 'tuning into' someone's voice is nearly impossible for me if there's a lot of background noise or loud music.

So, when in noisy environments, such as a pub or a party, it's not unusual for me to have a five-minute conversation with someone, finish it politely and have no idea who I was speaking to. "Not a friggin' clue". It's quite an art form. If you met me recently and found our conversation interesting because, I answered all your questions, there's a definite possibility that I didn't have a clue who you were... Sorry. This was because I couldn't hear what you asked, so I said something like, "Yes, definitely," and "That's great!" whilst nodding emphatically. I then ask open questions, which permit a long answer. These questions have other follow up questions that are valid, regardless of what the other person says. A five-minute conversation in the bag! I suppose it's disingenuous to a degree, but it's considerably more polite and less embarrassing than saying, "By the way, who are you?" after three or four minutes of otherwise pleasant chat.

Just so you know, I can confirm that 'definitely' is a very handy word. It doesn't say anything other than to agree with the person you're speaking to.

"Isn't that movie great/terrible?"

"Definitely."

"Don't you love/hate it when such and such happens?"

"Definitely."

"Hasn't the weather been great/terrible?"

"Definitely."

"Do you like my hair/dress?"

"Definitely."

It rarely lets me down.

But, there's an extreme example of these strategies failing hilariously. It's a cock-up of the highest order relating to girls. It involves hookers and a place in Singapore affectionately known, in Singapore, as the 'Four Floors of Whores' (Grandma, you know the drill. Oh, and Nick's new fiancé, perhaps best if you skip this bit too. He's a great catch, by the way).

Here goes...

A peculiar and frustrating chain of events during my Master's degree meant that I ended up on a flight to Singapore to see an old friend. It *began* with my study tour of South Africa. When we returned to Heathrow, we realised British Airways had left my wheelchair in Cape Town. This is the equivalent of having your legs chopped off, as it is the sole basis of my mobility. BA didn't get this. They lent me a standard chair that you see at airports, and I had to stay in London for the night while we waited for mine. Wheelchairs are like shoes - using one not designed for you quickly becomes painful. The next day, after much faffing on the phone, I was told that my chair was *still* in Cape Town.

Fantastic.

Exhausted, in pain, and more than a little frustrated, I made my way back to the comfort of my own home in York. The following day, I was overjoyed to hear that my wheelchair had arrived in London. We confirmed our address and waited with eager anticipation for it to be driven up to York. We waited. And waited. At about 7p.m. I finally got a call from the delivery guy who was confused about the directions to our house. A short, bizarre conversation led to the conclusion that the directions we were giving him bore no relation to where he actually was. It turned out he was in Surrey, a mere 230 miles away. BA had given him the wrong address.

Fantastic. Again.

I was reunited with my chair a mere *five days* after I had last seen it. As you would expect, British Airways took this matter very seriously. They offered me... drum roll... a £75 flight voucher.

There then followed an entertaining process of escalation, culminating in a personal letter from Willie Walsh (the BA Chairman), basically saying they were shit. He eventually offered two return tickets to anywhere on the BA network. Jackpot.

I used them to go to Singapore with Matty. I was interested to see it from a development perspective. It had transformed itself from one of the poorest nations in the 1960's, to become one of the richest. Also, and perhaps more importantly, I wanted to see an old friend, Nick Cheadle. Nick was a Resident Graduate at Bootham School and my first *ever* PA. The 'Res Grads' system basically gave university graduates a temporary job offering a bed and sub-minimum wage, a sort of post-higher-education sweatshop.

Nick had moved to Singapore with his wife, now ex. Whilst there, I also met up with my old Bootham history teacher, Max Hull. We met for dinner for what turned out to be his forty-second birthday. About half-way through what had become a very pleasant evening, my phone rang.

Nick: "Fraser, it's Nick. Late notice I know, but it's a boys night out... I have a green light, lets go!"

Me: "I can't Nick. I'm out with Max Hull."

He then whined and pleaded for about five minutes.

Nick: "OK *fine*. Late start then. When you're finished let me know and book a taxi to Orchard Towers, I'll meet you guys there."

We finished our evening with Max and his wife and returned to the hotel. At about 11p.m., Matty and me went to reception to order a taxi. The porter was a slightly creepy old guy with a very distinctive crooked, toothless smile and well-worn uniform. He looked about seventy going on a hundred-and-two. He overheard us ask for Orchard Towers. With his half smile in place, and with furtive hesitation, he said "Have a good night gentlemen… maybe you bring back lady?" His meaning would soon become clear to us.

We pulled up at Orchard Towers, Nick strode over to our taxi and, with a sweeping gesture, announced, "Gentlemen, I give you the *Four Floors of Whores*!" It turned out that Orchard Towers is a four-story brothel bar. Now, I must say that Nick is not a pervert or a 'user' of such facilities, his focus was purely a lads 'cultural education'. As we entered, a chubby five-foot man was exiting with a tall leggy girl. As he passed us he tapped me on the shoulder, "You're going have a lot of fun tonight kid." His hand was sweaty and soft, like a fat slimy toad. Creepy, nasty, sleazy, dirty bastard. We were going where he just came from. Oh dear.

The bars on each floor were themed; Wild West, beach bar, and other unimaginative clichés. The real challenge for me was to avoid eye contact with the girls. I'm self-conscious at the best of times, but it was clear that it was my western face, not the wheelchair, which was the real draw on this occasion. I could see that the slightest eye contact with a girl resulted in her coming over and chatting, offering lap dances and (probably) shags. I decided on a 'no-eye-contact' policy.

As we went through the bars, I used the same conversation technique I described above, generally chatting garbage with the lads and drinking beer. As yet, I'd avoided any girl-chat. I was prepared though… I needed to be careful. I couldn't deploy my trusted "Yes definitely, that's great," tactic. "Definitely!" was definitely not going to work on this occasion. Not in this bar. The resulting confusion would take too much explaining. I also had to remember not to say "Yes" either. The script I decided on was to say, "Nope! Not tonight! You're very nice though!" as loudly and clearly as possible, while firmly shaking my head until the girl got the message. Not particularly charming, but I figured it would get the job done with minimal embarrassment.

After an hour or so, we got in the lift for the top floor – the 80's bar. We knew the music would be shit, but I hadn't anticipated how loud it would be, it was the loudest yet.

As expected, my no-glance policy eventually failed. I thought I was staring at nothing in particular, but it turned out I was staring directly into the eyes of a pretty hooker. She had a tight micro skirt on, barely not naked. She was talking to my friend Matty and then came over to talk to me. I later learnt she was actually a really nice girl who had come over for a pick-up chat but realised we were not 'punters' in the sense she'd hoped for. Either through genuine interest (or *perhaps* a change of strategy) she began talking more genuinely to the guys and joining in with our conversation.

But, crucially, at the time I didn't know this. With Belinda Carlisle's 'Heaven is a Place On Earth' blasting out, the hooker came up to me. She said something in my ear. I steeled myself, drew breath and fired out, "NOPE. NOT TONIGHT. YOU'RE VERY NICE THOUGH."

I congratulated myself on having handled a potentially tricky and embarrassing situation rather well. It had the desired result and she hastily left me alone. Turns out I was wrong, as I discovered when Nick, who had overheard the question, revealed it to me: "So I hear you are studying politics and interested in Singapore?"

I have no game, not even with hookers.

Being more serious now, as I've said, my FA problems mean

that I need to pay a great deal of attention to communication. My speech is slurred, my eyesight is poor and my hearing is pretty ropey. I've had to take responsibility for my situation and look for ways to deal with it. I'll now share some more of them.

I've learnt to communicate only in environments where I can see and be heard. I used to struggle in noisy bars and echoey restaurants. Now I go to quieter bars and am more likely to have people over for dinner. My friends are more likely to suggest 'dinner and drinks at my place' rather than a busy bar in the city. When they come over I leave the lights on a little brighter. When I'm out, I generally try to sit with my back to the windows so that peoples' faces are not in shadow. When these things are not in place, I still enjoy socialising. If we're out in a dark, noisy bar or party, then I'm likely to just have an evening of enjoying the vibe, saying 'definitely' a lot and maybe cutting it short. These are solid controlling actions that give me the platform to communicate effectively and still have a good time when I can't communicate so well.

I've also learnt to speak very concisely. I choose my words carefully and then say them as clearly as possible. When I'm not heard, I repeat them until they are. Speech therapy and other breathing techniques have helped, but the main thing is being concise.

When preparing a speech or presentation, there is an old adage that you should speak the spoken word not the written world. Adrian and other great speakers sound natural and engaging. This holds particular relevance for me, as there is a massive difference between my spoken word and my written word. My written sentences can be as long as I want, but my limited lung capacity and control means that I tend to *speak* in much shorter sentence structures. So, a speech I've written would sound terrible if I then read it. I know, I've tried it. Saying this though, the difference between my spoken and written word has lessened in recent years. My reduced typing speed means that I've become as concise with the words I choose to write as the words I speak. Nonetheless, the spoken vs. written rule still applies, they're different.

Adrian was great at speaking. He was particularly good at tailoring what he said to his audience. An example of this was a series of meetings where he was introducing the Development Leadership Program. In the talks where other academics were present he'd use academic jargon to make his point; it was a jargon-relevant environment. When we met with a group that consisted of non-academics, Adrian covered the same ground but elegantly dropped the jargon and used normal terminology. It wasn't dumbing-down, it was about getting his point across. Everyone heard what he meant without needing to internally translate anything. Same meetings, different attendees, different communication strategy.

In this way, when not being rude to hookers, I've tried to do a lot of the things we've talked about in this book. That is, to look for ways to fix, control or compromise and never 'just accept' anything. Most of all, I feel like I've taken responsibility for things.

So much so that I've gone a stage further and now really enjoy public speaking. Looking back, it stems from Adrian's lectures I first heard when I was nineteen. My first real stab at it was at my twenty-first birthday party, when Jimmy 'interviewed' me. It was great fun and a serious thrill.

Public speaking is great. You command the attention of everyone in the room and they have to listen to you – i.e. monologue is best. It prevents long drawn out boring conversations. In addition to the various presentations I did for work, I've been invited to give speeches at my old school, at a primary school in Whistler, as a best man and as an after-dinner speaker at the gala dinners that follow the more-or-less-annual charity 'Big Bad Bike Rides' my dad organises.

The reason I like public speaking is because it's a very practical way for me to speak to lots of people at once. I find it a struggle to get to speak to everyone at a big party, but on my twenty-first birthday, I knew I'd spoken to everyone. Also, I get a lot of 'should have, would have' moments in conversations. With public speaking I can prepare and rehearse so that at least I get my point across as clearly as possible. Whilst I enjoy the applause, it's a satisfying way of communicating.

So that's Communication. I've talked about my challenges with it and a few of the strategies I've used to overcome some of my limitations. In addition, of course, I've been able to talk about a major source of inspiration in my life, Adrian. In my opinion, some of the lessons I learnt from him are universal ones. These include, *inter alia*, being objective, concise, and having the ability to listen with courtesy and sincerity. What Adrian did was to hugely accelerate what I was just beginning to get my head around anyway.

By way of eulogy for Adrian, I defer to someone else. Namely, Steve Hogg, the other main man at the Development Leadership Program. Steve's eulogy is a beautifully representative piece, which can't be improved on. Below are the first two paragraphs (Hogg, 2013). You'll notice I'm using the Harvard referencing system throughout the book. Ado would have gone mental otherwise.

In Tribute to Adrian Leftwich

1940 - 2013

It is with profound sadness that the Developmental Leadership Program (DLP) team advises you of the recent death of Adrian Leftwich, our inspirational Director of Research and the heart and soul of DLP and our politics-leadership-development work. Most importantly, at this difficult time the DLP team's thoughts and support are with Adrian's two wonderful children, Maddy and Ben.

As a highly regarded political scientist, and through DLP and its predecessors, Adrian has influenced development thinking internationally. His work through DLP contributed significantly to both UK and Australian development thinking, policies and programs, and his impact can also been seen elsewhere, for example with stakeholders such as the international Development Assistance Committee (DAC). We're confident that Adrian achieved his ambition to challenge and influence international aid orthodoxy: across the board, international aid agencies now recognise and better understand the centrality and complexity of politics in development, the political dynamics of economic growth, and role of local power and leaderships in legitimate institutional change. Adrian's work contributed to these achievements in no small measure. Few individuals can lay claim to such a contribution and it is a sign of Adrian's intellect and global influence that we can state it so confidently here."

Please take the time to read the rest of this eulogy at http://www.dlprog.org/about-us/adrian-leftwich/tribute-to-adrian.

php.

From Steve's words, I think you'll see that it wasn't just me who thought Ado was an impressive guy.

Chapter 6

Tiny Little Steps: Small steps lead to huge changes

Let's start here with the end. In the previous chapter, I mentioned that I travelled to South Africa on a study tour, in order to meet and interview a number of political elites and academics for my Master's degree dissertation. My thesis question was, 'Did the Truth and Reconciliation Commission create a reconciled polity in post-apartheid South Africa: is democracy sustainable?'. It allowed me to approach lots of different people, and made me riveting company in the pub.

So riveting, in fact, that it meant a random person in South Africa chatted me up…

My good school friend Mathew was my PA for the trip to South Africa. Over the years 'Matty' had, intermittently, been one of my main PAs when he didn't have a job. After several days of travelling, interviewing and writing up notes, we decided to take the day off.

There was a massive shopping mall near our hotel where we

ended up having a couple of beers. Matty excels in drinking and talking about sausages. In fact he's a sausage baron in Brighton, where he owns a deli-butchery. On this occasion, I chose the drinking option, as his enthusiastic sausage chat can be a bit tiresome. There was a big capoeira martial arts show on, with hard-core kung fu guys dancing around and looking like they were beating the shit out of each other, although they weren't. It was impressive.

Matty was fumbling around looking for his lighter, as he does frequently, when a chap came over and gave him a light. After a while we all got chatting and we soon moved on to my (obviously riveting) research topics and dissertation. The stranger seemed genuinely intrigued by my interest in the prospects of his country's democracy. All innocuous pleasant chat until, the conversation took a sordid turn.

I turned to him and asked, "What do you do for work?"

He looked back and said, "Oh me? I'm in the sex industry."

This is a standard response Dad gives at dinner parties, so I took it as a joke.

I replied with, "OK, so what have you been doing recently?"

"Well, last night I had two clients to pick up from the airport... I ended up having sex with the male client and his partner was watching and wanted to get involved..."

I was not expecting this.

"Ok right, erm..."

"But I am thinking about getting out of the prostitution bit and doing more pimp work, you know, running my own brothel. But mine will be particularly well-designed and thought out. A good environment for the girls to work in. I'm all for employment rights, you see."

I could only reply with, "I see."

With half a beer left and time to kill, I scratched my head

and took off my shades, putting them on the table (They were frameless Oakley Compulsives. It's difficult keeping up with the latest fashions, but I try).

The guy stopped mid-sentence and turned to look at me directly. "Oh my, you have beautiful blue eyes. Your eyes are dreamy."

At this point everything went slightly surreal, he wouldn't stop staring at me, his voice went all soft and he started biting his lip. Now I don't wish to appear prudish, but the combination of the heat, the beer and the rapid moves of a gay porn actor putting the heat on me was a little out of my comfort zone. I was beginning to think he wasn't actually that interested in my politics thesis either!

Now I know how girls feel when they get perved at.

I put my shades back on, quickly finished my beer, and made an excuse that we *had* to meet someone at the hotel. I gave Matty the universal 'Let's get the fuck out of here' sign. It's a subtle but intense look that's hard to misinterpret. Matty is not one to waste a pint but luckily he can down a drink in two seconds.

You learn new things every day.

My interviews were not with sex people, but politicians and political scientists, who had a range of perspectives about the sustainability of democracy. On my own and with Adrian's help, I managed to compose a pretty decent list of people to speak to. Damn good actually, if I say so myself.

One of the contacts I managed to secure was Vern Harris, a senior member of the Nelson Mandela Institute. Our interview was at their headquarters, itself a pretty frickin' cool experience. When we finished, Harris said he'd come with Matty and me back to the entrance to say goodbye. As we were walking along the corridor he stopped and said, "Hang on a minute." He knocked and opened a door to an office. It was Nelson Mandela's. Sadly he wasn't in. Whether this was because he was in a meeting or gone to lunch, I don't know. I hear he was gutted – but I left him some top tips about politics.

There were other interesting interviews too. I spent an enjoyable forty-five minutes with Desmond Tutu. He had the cheek to reject my first request. His secretary said he was too busy. But while I was in Johannesburg, she called me and said that 'Des' had read my email and said he'd like us to meet! This required a flight back to Cape Town, but it was worth it. I tend not to get star-struck, however, meeting someone who has made such a big difference in an area I value so highly was quite something. I was a little lost for words.

Adrian's connections also got me an interview with Albie Sachs, a high court constitutional judge. He helped write the South African constitution with Nelson Mandela and Oliver Tambo. I remember his handshake, it was quite unusual. Specifically, it was with his left hand, the right arm having been blown off in a car bomb attack in the late 80's by someone not so keen on ending apartheid. The blast also resulted in him losing the sight in his right eye. None of this stopped him in his work. *Properly* brave in my book – talk about volition.

This whole experience gave me a huge, 'how the hell have I got myself here?!' feeling. Five years previously, I was bemoaning the lack of wardrobe space in my undergrad student accommodation and here I am, just missing an opportunity to have a casual chat with arguably the greatest human being of modern times. For all I know, just because he'd gone to take a leak.

Another was my trip to the World Bank HQ I mentioned earlier. On the first morning, it became clear that getting into this bank wasn't as simple as entering any other bank I'd been into. It's as difficult as getting into an international flight terminal, only *more* tedious. After clearing security, we received 'I'm not a terrorist' ID badges on lanyards. Upon entering, I was surprised by the grandeur. The atrium was a gargantuan space of glass and steel in which people walked about looking important and wearing $3,000 suits. Evidently, they understood the dynamics of poverty. Apart from being impressed with the suitability of my wardrobe choices, I felt seriously out of my depth ("What the hell am I doing here again Jimmy?").

These stories both bring me on to Tiny Little Steps.

When I think about it, absolutely everything I've ever done has been a series of tiny little steps.

These progressed from getting over my wardrobe crisis, to attending lectures, writing essays and taking exams. Later, it was things like going to South Africa the first time to decide if my MA was something I really wanted to do. After being accepted and deciding to go for it, I realised I wanted to change to a part-time course as I needed (and *wanted*) more time to focus on my studies. This meant I could travel more, making the South Africa trip possible. That trip began with loads of emails and phone calls to find interviewees.

Then it gets awesome. The South Africa trip not only gave me the material I wanted to produce a dissertation I was proud of, it also cemented my relationship with Adrian. This formed the basis of my career that followed, including presenting at the World Bank HQ.

The dots connect nicely, but at no point are they that far apart, just Tiny Little Steps. The process of getting over a wardrobe storage crisis, to meeting Des (and nearly meeting Nelson) was a function of a great chain of events. The only thing that ties them all together is that they are the sum total of a long chain of small actions and events.

This came to mind when Jimmy and I discussed my speech for the Big Bad Bike Ride party in 2013. These bike rides are the best analogy I can think of for tiny little steps. Rather like the 'Nelson' story, I'll start at the end. To date, the rides have raised over £960,000 for the medical research work of Ataxia UK. This charity researches the disease and offers respite assistance for people with FA and other ataxias. In addition, the rides help hundreds of people keep fit, for at least part of the year, and it's a bloody good laugh. They also got my dad an MBE.

When I spoke about this remarkable achievement, I recalled how the £800k, the total amount raised at that point, didn't happen overnight. In fact, it had taken twenty-two years. The first ride raised £20k and it's gone steadily up and up. The 2014 ride eventually hit £140k from four hundred riders. In 2013, it raised £75k with ninety-seven riders. Although all the rides are put together by my dad, a major achievement in itself, the riders' successes aren't one man's effort, but that of the hundreds and hundreds of people who completed them.

For my speech, I decided to take the argument a bit further. From one perspective the riders don't 'just ride' 100km, a 100km ride is more easily achieved by riding 1km a hundred times. The only thing that would stop this whole thing happening was if anyone at any point *stopped* taking tiny little steps. Nobody does. Riders of all shapes and sizes endure what, for many, is the toughest physical challenge they face all year. The sports riders fly around and have a great 'ride out'. The bike rides, however, aren't actually designed for them, they're for the *non*-riders. My dad has focused on this group. The majority of the logistical work involved is there to help them get around. They're the ones who push themselves to the absolute limit and who deserve the greatest respect. After all, they have to try their hardest for longest. And they do it by taking tiny little steps, pedalling and pedalling all day long.

And it isn't the hundreds of riders who donate the money; it comes from the *thousands* of people that sponsor them. Each little click for each little, sometimes huge, donation all added up to something which landed my dad in Buckingham Palace chatting to Princess Anne. Queen 'Liz' is normally there to give out national honours. She was obviously gutted to miss the opportunity to meet my dad, but she had already said she'd go to Canada, a rare scheduling error by the Palace.

Dad had the vision for the rides and made the dream a reality. It *is* his achievement. However, it was the thousands of tiny little steps by thousands of people that led him to his own 'what the hell?' feeling as we entered the gates to Buckingham Palace. In fact, we all had that feeling.

Buckingham Palace was quite an interesting place to hang out in for the morning. For the big day, my parents invited: me to represent the kids, Grandma to represent the family, and Jimmy to represent the hundreds of people who have helped Rebecca and me over the years.

The first thing we learnt is that Buckingham Palace isn't particularly palace-like in places. The ceremony is held in the Ballroom on the first floor, so you need to get upstairs. Luckily Liz had thought of this and has had a lift installed (a nasty cheap one. She isn't one to waste taxpayers' money). To get to it, one of the ushers took Jimmy and me through an anonymous door into the backstage areas with worn carpet and generally clean but functional surroundings. It was like the behind the scenes area of a posh hotel; this is where the elves work. Once on the first floor, the door opens and 'bang', you're back in palace land.

Mum liked Buckingham Palace because the loos had swanky handles and the floors were so shiny even she approved. It was the closest she's come to being in as clean a place as our home. Mum likes swanky things and shiny handles, and cleanliness. She likes these things a lot.

A lot of people from the Inland Revenue got honours (it must be the noble work they do). There was also a lady who got an honour for services to tattooing. Apparently, she helps people who are disfigured by ailments. For example, women who've had to have a mastectomy due to breast cancer lose their nipple, so she uses her talents to create a realistic replacement. Clever tattoo lady. The coolest guy was a forces chap we decided to call Flash Gordon. He received an award to mark his leadership in battle. You could hear every last woman in the audience sigh as he strutted up in his hyper-cool uniform, like at a boy band concert, but more prim and proper.

It was an amazing experience and I felt very proud. As we had our photograph taken in the courtyard, the press were all over Flash Gordon. We were sitting next to his dad during the ceremony. Apparently his son had lost a lot of men in a battle and was heroic in getting the rest out. Cool bastard, another properly brave hero.

Moving back to Tiny Little Steps.

I think I've learnt a bit about this through dealing with my health. There's lots of things wrong with me, most of which are getting worse. My girl chat is pretty much screwed, but a lot else is still working! Each time a new challenge comes along, fixing it is often pretty straightforward. For example, when I found it more difficult to walk longer distances in my early teens, it was *obvious* that the easier way to get about was to use a wheelchair. That wasn't rocket science.

However, this hasn't always been the case. Sometimes it's taken ages before we pin down exactly what the problem is. Like when I started getting knackered at the gym, Jimmy suggested Powerade, which made me feel worse. Because we didn't know I was diabetic, the chosen course of action was in fact the *worst* thing to do. It was a small step in precisely the wrong direction. It was the diagnosis that released me to get back to normal life.

In more recent years, I was becoming absolutely exhausted most of the time. I tried working less, tweaking my insulin dosages, drinking less coffee, but I still felt knackered. Eventually, we found that I had developed a thyroid problem. But there's medication available and, after a bit of trial and error, I was pretty close to feeling normal again.

A year ago, I felt like I had jet-lag every day. I'd wake up at stupid hours and find it difficult to get back to sleep. I tried going to bed earlier/later, staying in bed later, napping in the afternoon, but I still couldn't get a decent amount of sleep. I'd spend a lot of time in bed, but it was mostly dozing, I'd rarely stay asleep for longer than an hour or two. It was even suggested, by my mum no less, that I reduce my gym time – an obscene proposition. The hospital gave me an oxygen monitor to sleep with. It showed that each time I fell asleep, my blood oxygen levels were dropping and my body would wake me up in order to re-oxygenate itself. It was happening four or five times a night, hence the short bursts of sleep. My impaired lung function meant that I wasn't getting enough oxygen when asleep and was missing the deep restorative sleep we all need. So, now I use a machine that gives me a Michael Jackson-esque dosage of oxygen. I feel a bit like Bane from The Dark Knight Batman film, but I get *proper* sleep. So, whilst it doesn't give me Tom Hardy's physique (God dammit), it does solve the problem.

This all has relevance to my mantras: 'never just accepting', 'taking responsibility', and 'control and compromise'.

Relating to this chapter... I've come to understand that it's very difficult to solve a problem if you can't identify it. You can't chuck solutions at a problem without knowing what the problem is. But chucking solutions and failing repeatedly ultimately *helps fix the problem*. This is huge for me, and it's not just relevant to the doom and gloom health stuff, not by any means.

For example, skiing, for *years* I struggled with my left turns. I was able to control and extend my rigger to the right without a problem, but my left turns were never as good. They always lacked consistency and were never as strong as my right turns. It became immensely frustrating, each lesson was punctuated with repeated conversations about how I needed to extend and rotate my left rigger further, at a better angle and with greater consistency. We tried adjusting my sit-ski straps and the lengths of my outriggers and even changing the way my hands were strapped to them. Still my left turns were a bit shit. One evening, I was doing some beef-caking (physio) in the hotel room. Jimmy and I noticed that, when I extend my arms out straight, my right arm appeared to be two inches longer than my left! The blinding flash of the obvious was that, while my back is perfectly straight, the original scoliosis meant that it was rotated a little bit. This meant I could reach further to the right than left. In fact, just enough to screw up my left turns. We fixed the problem with my left turns by adding additional padding behind my left shoulder in the sit-ski. Finding the problem, and facing it, overcame the challenge more or less instantly. We ended up there by failing, failing and failing again, until we cracked it.

Of course, this is an old adage, 'finding the problem is half the solution'. Nonetheless, I feel I have Adrian to thank for really understanding what this means. Adrian showed me the importance of thinking objectively to really understand any problem. By doing so, I'm able to keep looking at things in new ways; not to do so would risk me going into the 'just accepting it' zone.

Another good example involves a relatively *tiny* thing, something no more complicated than my feet slipping off my wheelchair footplate. It would happen now and then, but it soon became a 'thing'. They were always slipping off. It went on for too long because I failed to acknowledge the problem. It was just the way things were. It was the moment when we decided to call it a problem that we fixed it. Jimmy got some bits from the hardware store and added them onto the existing footplate. We only fixed it when we decided it was a problem, when we looked at it objectively. Before that it was just a pain in the arse. I've since had a proper new footplate made and it's as if the problem was never there.

Being able to look objectively is not just about fixing problems. It's often the source of finding entirely new opportunities too. Glen, the WASP instructor who helped me get up Spanky's Ladder, has another passion in life – kite surfing.

When I was in Canada in 2014, he suggested I have a go. I always figured he liked kite surfing because he can do it in board shorts while surrounded by hot girls in bikinis. But apparently it was good fun too. What was clear to me was that Glen had taken the skills he's learnt at Whistler Adaptive Ski Program and transferred them to this entirely different sport. He knew what I was capable of, and that I'd flown big stunt kites and done paragliding before. Instead of the normal surfboard arrangement, he rigged a kite onto a small dingy and strapped me into a comfortable position. Essentially, he removed the balance element from kite surfing but kept the rest. It was excellent fun; kind of like skiing, being powered along by the elements, but by wind rather than gravity. I was fully engaged and involved, but with my limitations dialled out through Glen's clever thinking. This objective thinking has resulted in an entirely new sport for me, and a new venture for Glen (Cue shameless plug - Adaptive Kite Sports Canada, www.adaptivekitesportscanada.com).

So, while the ability to think objectively is something I've enjoyed getting my head around and using to positive effect in life, I've also learned to really appreciate seeing it in others.

The other thing I feel I've learnt is that the first steps are often the most difficult. They can seem ridiculous and pointless and the chance of failure might appear way too high.

An example for me is my journey into the gym. The weights I was initially lifting were pathetically small. Then again, this was after my back op and I weighed 6 stone (38kg / 84lb). Those initial steps were horrible and the goal, to get fit, looked ridiculous. But in time things improved and the weights went up and up. Then my skiing trips asked new challenges of me, a big one was the need to get my 'core working'. I've never really thought about my core before. Kevin, one of my physiotherapists, knew the dynamics of my body and had the medical insight to understand what my specific challenge was.

He got me to try various things involving balance and coordination. The calling cards of FA, amongst other things, are shit balance and coordination. My first attempts were atrocious, I simply couldn't do them at all and flopped about. But in time the strength came and I was balancing better. These core exercises are now a staple part of my sessions with Gym Weapon Mark.

In fact, at the time of writing I have *just* achieved another goal I set myself two years ago. That was to weigh more, 70kg to be precise. Ever since my back op, I was focused on getting fitter and stronger. Seventy kilograms was a pipe dream so it wasn't really a goal. My starting point was 38kg after all. However, two years ago, my annual hospital weigh-in showed me that I'd hit 63.8kg. So, I set a goal of 70kg for the next weigh-in and worked hard towards it. It wasn't a case of just eating more pies and cake. It was a case of more gym work, good diabetes control, good food and plenty of protein shakes. A year later, I went to the weigh-in and had hit 67.3kg. At this point I thought I wouldn't be able to do it, I was maxing out on everything I could do and nothing was changing. I was happy that I'd taken things as far as I could but a little disappointed that the 70kg eluded me. I'd hit my natural balance.

I continued at the same rate and, of critical importance, I started using a new piece of equipment that helps me exercise my legs. It's a sort of semi-powered cycle-action rig. Frank, my most recent main PA and fitness expert, worked out a series of adaptations that meant I could use it effectively. This has been a revelation for me, as I am now able to exercise a part of my body that was otherwise a no-go area. The knock-on effect? At my last weigh-in I was 70.1kg. This might not sound like a big deal for most people, but it was for me.

Could I have found this solution ten years ago? Yes. Am I

bothered it's taken me so long? No. I've found it at last. Simple things make me happy.

As I've said, it's usually the *first few* steps that are often the most difficult when taking on a new challenge. In fact, if they aren't then you might need to question the goal.

This has huge relevance to the journey Jimmy and I have taken to write this book. The process we've used has been as follows:

- We made *lots* of notes.
- We discussed the material and decided on a structure.
- Each note section and story was allocated to a chapter.
- Jimmy then wrote the chapter.
- I reviewed it.
- We both went through it and made changes until it was something we felt looked 'finished'.
- We submitted this to Lisa Chaney, our executive editor, who would read it, and we'd meet without Jimmy. This helped her get to know *me* better.
- She'd make suggested amendments and give us tips and thoughts on what we were doing right and wrong. But we weren't to go back and make these amends yet, she instructed us always to keep going forward.
- So, we would move onto to the next chapter and Jimmy would start writing again.
- Once we finished the book, Jimmy was finally able to go back and put all of Lisa's amends and structural corrections in place. At this point, Jimmy learnt the value of the comma!
- At the same time, Jimmy and I read through the entire thing, made changes we thought it needed and tried (often in vain) to answer questions Lisa had posed in her notes.

- We gave the whole thing to her again for her to read through.
- The final step, which at the time of writing we haven't done yet, will be to read through the whole book with Lisa, to turn our ramblings into something readable.
- (In fact, all three of us are just reviewing this chapter and can tell you it's been a – frequently hilarious – marathon!)

Quite a few little steps. At times, it has felt like a never-ending story for all of us. Particularly for me. But as Jimmy is typing this sentence as part of our final edit (in Portugal naturally), it's feeling nearly done.

The first chapter review with Jimmy shook my confidence a lot. I objected strongly to large sections of it and we ended up going over and over it to get something we agreed on – it took an age. But, in time, we've learnt what we're doing. I became more comfortable with sticking my neck out and Jimmy became better at sticking it out for me. It's become a dance of sorts. From Jimmy's perspective, he learnt better how to do this and my confidence in him has grown. We now both really look forward to our chapter review meetings.

The guiding hand here has been Lisa, who has shepherded us through this process. Although the process was at first fraught and difficult, she knew exactly what we were going through. The frustrations and challenges were new to Jimmy and me, but they weren't new to her. She knew exactly what we were getting ourselves (blindly) into. We've become better writers, and I've become a better listener! Lisa's knowledge and guidance only revealed itself to us gradually. The difficult few steps we had were not just something we would overcome but have become part and parcel of what it takes to write, what we hope, is a half-decent book. This 'dance' is something we talk a lot more about in the final chapter. The point here is, that (although we didn't let on to Lisa) the first few steps were awful.

So, in truth, the shaky start should have made me feel quietly relieved, because I would have realised that this goal *is* big enough. Of course it was difficult to do at the time, that's because we'd set a big fat goal.

To summarise Tiny Little Steps, the lessons for me are fivefold:
- Taking tiny little steps in the wrong direction isn't necessarily a bad thing. They can be a good thing. Knowing what something isn't, helps you find out what it is.
- The really important thing is to take the steps. Not taking steps means nothing happens and you get stuck with problems that invariably get in your way more and more.
- It's important not to regret the time it takes to fix a problem. Once it's fixed, I try to move on and don't dwell on the ridiculous path I may have taken to get there. It's done, move on.
- The first few steps are often the most difficult. In fact, if they are not then it might be worth checking the goal – chances are it might not be big enough.
- Try to avoid taking any steps that result in fancying girls made of cardboard.

Looking beyond my limitations is where it begins, actually making it happen is the process of these tiny little steps.

I'll finish this chapter by talking about my dad again. Prior to the London Olympics he was asked to carry the Olympic torch in Harrow, a suburb of London. A couple of my friends lived in the area so went down to wish him well and take the obligatory Facebook pics to share with everyone. Sure enough several pictures appeared on Facebook with my dad tagged... along with me, Mum, Rebecca, Sophie and Lucy. This was peculiar because, at the time, Rebecca and I were in York and Mum was in Portugal with Sophie and Lucy.

It turned out that my dad had picked up the torch from an Indian guy in a wheelchair. Everyone assumed it was me and the rest of the family were with me. What I should explain at this point is that, over the years I've developed a dedicated focus on getting tanned, I'm known for my 'sexy-beasting' efforts. It makes me attractive and debonair looking. In fact, I missed my dad's torch carrying because I was catching a flight later that day in order to catch some rays. Of course, the key to a good tan is tiny little steps, so to be compared so favourably to a man sporting such a deep and natural colour, well, it brings a tear to me eye.

Lets move on to the last chapter. It's the most important one in the book.

Chapter 7

Trust in Others: Putting your trust in others and saying 'yes'.

This chapter is the one that I've been focussing on from the beginning. It's what everything else is based on and allows me to offer thanks and appreciation to those who have helped me, without having to sneak them in here and there as I've had to so far. I hope you appreciate now, that it's central to everything I do. This chapter is also intended to summarise everything else that's come before. To 'tell you what I've tried to tell you', so to speak.

A big lesson, for me, is realising, once again, how everything is context-specific. Forgive me for geeking out a bit here, but I'm going to plunge into academia, specifically politics. The point is that politics isn't really about philandering politicians kissing babies while peddling fudged figures. It's really about understanding context and how it's different for everything and everyone. Politics is everywhere. It was Adrian, in particular, that I credit with this understanding (Leftwich,

2004). He taught me that there is no universal blueprint when approaching problems of political development. One particular academic paper Adrian and Steve Hogg wrote describes this perfectly (Leftwich and Hogg, 2008); they described how efforts to reform the developing world often fail because the international community simply repeats what had worked somewhere else. The problem is that this sort of 'top down mono-cropping' doesn't take into account the context of the country – it's history, culture, traditions, laws and customs. Adrian explained that the only way to create effective change was through a 'bottom-up', context-specific approach.

In this respect, I've tried to offer *my* context. If it's to be of any value to anyone else, then they need to see their challenges through their own eyes. I'm just me; I don't pretend to be anything else. All problems are unique to each particular situation. Indeed, Adrian consistently reinforced this in the academic sphere, but he knew (as he was clever and wise) that this is applicable to any challenge in life. No problem has the same solution. Everything is particular to your own circumstances.

I hope it's been clear that we haven't pretended to offer anything new - I'm not that clever! I don't pretend for a second that I've handled my challenges brilliantly. I'm forcefully reminded of this because, as we begin this chapter, I'm nursing a fractured knuckle after slamming my fist when frustrated with my computer mouse. It was me versus the table; the table won and my hand hurts. Nonetheless, what I hope I've done is show some of the ways I've interpreted some of my own context-specific challenges. Perhaps this will prompt you to the odd thought. Even if it doesn't, it's been an enjoyable experience for me to reflect on things and try and put everything down on paper.

One thing I've talked about, given credit to, and based entire chapters on, is other people.

At last I'm able to talk more about other people, specifically the trust I put in them. Hundreds of people are massively relevant to this chapter. I will cover several here but want all of them (you) to know that if you *think* you are relevant to this chapter then please understand that you *are*.

I put an awful lot of trust in other people. I have to. I also *enjoy* the process. The specific need I have to trust people, hopefully, allows me to talk about it in a new and interesting way.

I wouldn't ask a lawyer to fix my car nor a mechanic to defend me in court. We're all inter-reliant on the help of others. In my case, the nature of the trust I put in others is more immediate and tangible. If you consider how much we *all* rely on the actions of others, then for me it's really a case of visibility and removal of privacy rather than any profound new concept.

We were all babies once, so we have all been entirely reliant on others. As we grow up, the normal progression is that this reliance diminishes and other peoples' reliance on us increases. This isn't necessarily the case for me. However, the kind of help I ask of others has definite boundaries, I may need a hand with eating or getting about, but I don't when it comes to the stuff of thought and mindset. I need to overcome physical challenges. Physical disability has set the rules of the game for me, but it is my responsibility to focus on what I can do.

And this is one of the fundamental themes of this book. When I rolled the sit-ski and scared the shit out of Jimmy, my mistake was that I didn't take responsibility for what we did and did not do. I put blind faith in others and didn't care. It was fun but not smart. As Adrian explained earlier, it was only when he learnt to take responsibility for everything that he could find his internal redemption. If it applies to sit-skiing and political activism, it applies everywhere!

This brings me onto my Personal Assistants (PAs). The process by which I learnt to put my trust in others was as natural and organic as it could possibly have been. As I've said before, in the beginning all of my 'PAs' were my school friends. When I needed help to carry something or a hand to hold when walking about, they would simply help like friends do. It was seamless. It was no big deal. When I got a class assistant to help with my books, word processor and note taking, it was much the same, an entirely normal and harmonious process. I imagine this is a function of my age at the time and the way children are naturally flexible and free-thinking.

As my reliance on the help of others increased, so did the need for my friends to make money. This was perfect. While they would help me anyway, now they could get paid for it. I suspect this mix of PAs being friends and getting paid meant that I didn't feel as disabled or compromised as I would have been if, say, I'd become reliant on wheelchairs later in life (such as by injury). This has given me specific cause for reflection. I feel fortunate that I haven't had to face immediate or particularly abrupt challenges with FA. Everything has happened relatively slowly. From my perspective, the progressive nature of my condition has made it slightly easier to deal with. This might be different from the way many people might think and feel. Given no alternative, they'd most likely rather be able bodied and then lose the ability to move about quite quickly, rather than to have it taken away from them slowly from a young age. From my perspective, the slow journey to where I am now has allowed me to fight, adapt, and compromise to every challenge that has got me here.

At the very start, it was just a case of mates helping mates like we'd always done. Friendship at the start, cash and friendship later. This has been a big lesson for me. I learnt early on that good friends make the best PAs. This was tested in my mid twenties when the availability of friends to work for me dried up. Their advancing careers and commitments meant they were less able to work PA hours for PA wages.

At this point, I began using a specialist agency that recruits, trains and allocates PAs to people who need them. This was a watershed moment, as I no longer relied on the organic friend-based system but instead on a formalised process where the PAs became employees. It was a frustrating process, but ultimately one that I had to undertake. The increasing practical difficulty of relying on friends had left me no choice. Also, by having my *own* PAs, I was gaining *independence*. The system of asking friends for help had long moved beyond the sweet spot where everyone wins. It had become one of the important wake-up calls that I've become familiar with in living with FA – things were changing. It required this subtle but very important perspective shift. What I'd learnt from hiring friends was, that PAs need to be mates. If they're not, they are just employees and that isn't good enough. It'd be shit. I need to live my life, not just sustain it. A good starting point is to surround myself with friends. As I spend more time with my PAs than anyone else, we must become friends if it's going to work.

So, I made a rule that my PAs in the future would always need to become good friends. It's non-negotiable and luckily I've attracted outstanding people around me. A huge lesson was realising that they didn't necessarily have to be *like* me. Some of the best and strongest carer-based friendships have been ones where they're totally different from me. You name it – nationality, interests, political views, sexual orientation, music taste (e.g. Dylan's ridiculous doom-metal), the lot.

Perhaps their *values* have always been in line with mine… or at least compatible. I can best describe my values as:

- Determination
- Tolerance
- Open-mindedness
- Thoughtfulness
- Love of adventure
- Loyalty
- Friendship

Other things that would feature on this list, if they were values, are enjoyment, fun and *belief*. I might not be the cleverest person in the world, far from it, but I've learnt that if you have belief in yourself then you can achieve an awful lot.

Again, this should sound familiar by now. I've tried to push my limits in everything I've done. How this came about is told within the stories of this book. This includes the numerous times when I've pushed it too far or gone about things the wrong way.

What's interesting to me are opportunities I've missed or didn't capitalise on because I was overwhelmed by something else. It happens to everyone and I definitely include myself here. For me, university, work, relationships and health, have all knocked me off track at times. They've swamped me, and all logic and rational thinking go out the window. During these periods I haven't been anywhere near 'the zone' of looking for new opportunities. I've been unwilling or unable to look for them, I've been consumed by something else.

Sometimes it's been a *worthy* distraction. The principle example being my FA-related health and wellbeing challenges. They can be all-consuming, and rightly so. It's been heavy shit at times and has demanded a lot of mental focus and fortitude.

Whilst I touched on Dark Times earlier in the book, and described how I don't get them a great deal, this doesn't mean I don't get them at all. In fact, there have been quite a few, just less than you might expect. I'm tempted to say that they all belong in the 'worthy distraction' category. Whilst some of them are FA-related, many have come about as a result of those episodes in life we all experience, those times where nothing beats experience. I'd handle them differently next time. Included in this category would be some disingenuous friendships and, I concede, the odd pretty girl.

Less productive times also include university essays. When I had a deadline, it might as well have been the end of the world, it could stop turning for all I cared. Nothing mattered whatsoever other than my hitting my word-count and making my Harvard references all neat and tidy.

Another was a particularly unsuccessful hair experiment. I attempted a hair dying manoeuvre, which was intended to thrust me to the pinnacle of fashion; others would drop to my feet in reverence. However, rather than creating a dynamic and utterly cool hairstyle, my hairdresser made me look like a bird had shat on my head. I can tell you that absolutely nothing happened until I returned the next day to have it fixed. Thankfully, they did a great job, disaster was averted.

What's worth acknowledging is that I haven't a friggin' clue what I could have done during these down times. How can I find new opportunities if I'm not looking for them? I don't worry for a second about what I 'should have / would have / could have' done during these periods, that's not me at all. It's still my responsibility to move on though. What's worked for me is trying to be objective and taking a step back to see myself from an abstracted position. To ask myself 'why am I doing this/feeling like this?'. Basically, to keep the stuff we've talked about in this book at the *front* of my mind.

It's like going to the gym. Unless I keep on with it, the benefits quickly disappear. And it's still happening. As I mentioned previously, in Canada in 2014 I tried kite surfing. It rocks.

The clear exception to all this was my hair disaster – nothing on earth was more important that day, and that's the truth, Obama would agree.

Without wishing to sound too cheesy, I must revert to the basic premise that *belief* matters. I'm not saying everyone can do everything brilliantly, in fact probably the opposite. But if you *believe* you can do something, then you more than likely *can* in one way or another... and you'll likely be much better than you'd otherwise be if you never tried in the first place. It starts with belief. Right on the tail of belief is perception, as one informs the other. If you believe in yourself then you perceive yourself differently.

I know, cheesy, but hear me out.

Very occasionally I've been asked, "How's life in a wheelchair?" I know a lot of people probably ponder the same question. My response could be, "How's life being butt ugly?" It's how you perceive your problems, not about the problems themselves. When people ask me what it's like being in a wheelchair, having metal in my back, not being able to do things, to me it's not a problem. *I just don't perceive it.* This is why I hate seeing myself on video. As I speak with Jimmy, discussing this paragraph, I feel I am speaking with absolute clarity. When I see a video, I can't stand it; I see how others might see me. This goes a long way to explaining the value of those who occupy my inner circle that you'll read about shortly – I believe they perceive me something like the way I perceive myself.

This is also why I enjoy talking to kids. *They* don't yet have so many preconceptions about the world. They don't care, they just do, they don't think of what can and can't be done or presuppose what compromises might bother me. It doesn't matter to them, like it doesn't to me, like it doesn't matter to my inner circle.

❦

Getting back to Trust in Others. Having PAs is actually quite cool. One aspect of having friends work for you, is the opportunity to live a life surprisingly free of the restrictions that many others are burdened with. If you wanted to go somewhere for a week or two with a friend, more often than not, they'll say they 'need to sort it out with work'. When your friend's job is *working for you*, then this problem disappears. At first, I didn't realise that this opened up new possibilities. With PAs as friends – friends first and paid second – the opportunities for adventure and travel are good. This began with Rory, Tom, Alex, George and Jimmy, when we went on a tour of the United States. From their perspective, they are *earning* while they travel so the trips become semi-funded for them. I'm very lucky to have travelled widely with friends. Then skiing happened, which eventually led to my epic round the world trip with G-Dog.

My travels only happen after making a conscious decision and saying 'yes let's do it'. This probably doesn't sound like anything new, everyone feels they decide to do something before doing it. My point is that it can be far trickier to get the option in the first place.

I tried to explain this with my 'Climbing the Ladder Sitting Down' letter to Cindy when skiing in Canada. I did nothing, it was James, Alex, Glen, Jimmy and all the strangers that made it happen. All I did was say 'yes', when I had the option to say 'no thanks'. It's a useful little word. But I only had the option to say it after a huge chain of events, tiny little steps even, requiring lots of self-belief. To arrive at the option in the first place was the challenge.

Another time I tried to explain this, was during an after-dinner speech I gave for one of the FA charity bike rides. *Everyone* in the room had said 'yes I'll do it'. They all had the much less arduous option of saying 'no thanks', but instead said 'yes'. The point is that whenever you are presented with the option to say 'no', that's it. Whatever was, will continue to be and nothing new happens. For the non-cyclists in the room, their decision to say yes is hugely the result of my dad. He's the one who helped them believe in themselves. All of his communications talk about how they *can* do it, and how much support they'll receive and how proud they'll be in completing the ride. The decision was a simple one, the process of gaining the belief and confidence to say 'yes' is a little more involved than one might expect. From a profoundly disabled guy's perspective, I can't emphasise how big a difference this has made to my life.

If you put your trust in others and say YES, more often than not, great things happen.

In mid-2014, the United Kingdom only just agreed to continue to be one nation. A referendum offering Scottish independence narrowly failed, and the UK will remain the UK (and rightly so in my opinion). The problem was that, for me, the campaign was based on a yes/no choice and the choice not to do something is much less spirited and exciting than the option to make something new happen. I called David Cameron to offer some tips on this; he didn't return my calls… the foolish toff, he nearly blew it.

I'd like to revisit the differentiation I make between trust and faith in Chapter 2. For great things to happen, it must be with someone you trust. If you do not have trust in them, then you are just rolling the dice.

Rolling the dice is of no interest to me for two reasons:
- First of all, it's just plain dangerous.
- Secondly, it's unfulfilling.

When you roll the dice you're leaving your actions to fate, you have no control. What's interesting to me is taking control of my life.

The enjoyment I derive from pushing my limits is a function of my involvement. When I ski I do so collaboratively. Same with paragliding, going to the gym, travel, kite surfing, socialising, having fun – *everything*. It's through trust that I can take part in these things effectively. But I must contribute in order to engage, otherwise I'm just going along for the ride, which would be boring and pointless. The best example I can give is my total disinterest in going bungee jumping. I've lost count of the number of times people have suggested it. Often they've done research into disabled bungee programmes and then proudly suggested it as 'my next extreme activity'. I politely refuse. The reason is that there is no collaboration, besides me handing over some cash and being pushed off a bridge. From my perspective and *context*, people like bungee jumping because it pushes their limits and requires them to put *blind* faith in someone else – playing with fate. These are precisely the reasons I have no interest in it.

There's never going to be an easy point to talk about this next paragraph, but now is as good a time as any and it's important I share it.

Perhaps unusually for my age, and as direct result of having Friedreich's Ataxia, I've had to face the ultimate fear on a few occasions. By this I mean the sense of possible death. I don't mean the calculated risk of my back operation. I'm talking about being caught out and finding myself in a position where I was alone, in need of assistance, unable to get it, and having a descending 'this is it, I could be about to die', feeling. On these occasions I had an extreme sense of absolute priorities. It's not been a case of my life flashing before my eyes, more a sense of absolute clarity about those I love, what I love doing and a deep sense of dissatisfaction that I won't die doing what I love.

Like I said before, I don't think I felt *personal* fear, more a sense of huge embarrassment and regret that I would be inconveniencing those around me so much. I know that sounds absurd, but I'm reporting honestly. The most unpleasant aspect of all these occasions was losing communication. In these circumstances, I lose ALL of it. Finding myself in a state of absolute aloneness, unable to speak to anyone, means I must be staring death in the face.

At the same time I have this strong sense of regret that I won't have told those I love how much I do. This horrible predicament, and how to deal with it is, as yet, a challenge I haven't resolved. The only solution I have is to avoid it at all costs.

You'll notice I haven't talked much about my future in this book. We've brushed by it a couple of times. But, actually, this is a fair representation of me. I'm comfortable in saying

I don't think much about the future. And I don't think I have a perverse aversion to what we all know to be true. That my life is affected by Friedreich's Ataxia doesn't make a huge difference here. We're all going to die – life is short for all of us. The one lesson I've learnt is to live life for the moment. Plan for the future? Of course. But dwell on it? No thanks. This isn't denial of my circumstances, it's called getting on with life.

I don't think I need to write any more about the importance of putting my trust in others. What I would like to do, though, is introduce you to some of them…

Inner Circle

Welcome to my inner circle. Well, chances are you're not in it; but welcome to the first time I've talked about it publicly. It's not a masonic club of corrupt, sinister, scheming thugs who are up to no good. It's actually just a group of people who I share my inner thoughts with.

Like many people, my close friendships started at school. In this respect I'd like to give credit to Bootham, a Quaker school in York. A central tenet of Quakerism is the idea of equality and mutual respect. Assemblies are held in silence and you sit in a quadrant with nobody sitting above anyone else, everyone is equal. The people running Bootham when I was there were exceptional in giving me the best chance of growing up feeling equal to my peers. I didn't see this at the time, I was too busy being a kid, but I understand it clearly now. The friends I met at school all came from backgrounds whose families identified with the ethos at Bootham. That's why their kids were there. I can't help thinking this is at least partly the reason I found such good people around me. This is irrespective of wealth too. At the time, the comprehensive scholarship and sponsorship system in place meant that my classmates came from a wide spectrum of backgrounds. What tied everyone together was the school, and for that I'm really grateful my parents sent me there.

My inner circle wasn't formed through any particular conscious thought; it was through absolute, unavoidable necessity. Nonetheless, I value it greatly. As my need to rely on others increased, so my inner circle developed.

My appreciation of close friendships is nothing new: a problem shared is a problem halved. Being objective and sharing feelings are both things we all understand and can, more often than not, practice a lot more than we do.

Having more than my share of problems, I'm forced to be more open, and many of the challenges I have are more apparent and visible. Put bluntly, when I have a personal problem I'd otherwise keep to myself, no joy, I'm forced to share it because there is no other way I can deal with it.

This section is not intended to be a gush-fest of thanks to my mates. The reason we've added it is to try and demonstrate 'Trust In Others' on a practical level. These are the people who've made so much of what I've talked about in this book a *reality*.

If you look at the chapter titles of this book, none of them would have made any difference to my life if I wasn't able to trust people. These people have made everything actually *happen*. It's been useful to refer to my disability throughout the book because I hope it's provided more interesting and compelling examples of how I've coped with serious challenges. But that was the 'hook'. What *really* matters is the way trusting others has given me far more than 'coping with being disabled'.

It's given me a genuinely thrilling existence.

There's a pretty wide spectrum of people in my inner circle, each one with his or her own particular qualities. This variety is a vital feature, making my inner circle so much more meaningful and useful to me. In a sense, through this variety, I'm able to see more perspectives and have specialists around me from lots of areas. If there's something I need advice on, there's always someone to call.

The Inner Circle is an amorphous bunch; there is no rank or order.

Here we go...

George: He's consistently the most unflappable person I've ever met, with self-deprecation in abundance. He has no shame and is hysterically entertaining. George has found a fantastic wife who has stunned us all with her ability to see his awesome qualities, despite his predilection to get naked in public at any opportunity. I gave his best man speech with our friend Alex, it pretty much wrote itself. I won't give details here but rest assured I ridiculed him sufficiently and, everyone in the room understood his nudist tendencies. His ability to make light of any situation and his kind heart is – like his back hair – large and impenetrable. I have never argued with George.

Alex: AKA 'BA', for no other reason than these are his initials spelt backwards, is a corporate whore par excellence. He was famous at school for starting big projects the day before the deadline and then getting better marks than the rest of us. These days he seems to spend most of his time 'turning left' as he boards long haul flights in expensive

With some hardcore instructors
in 2012, Glen, Doug and James.

With Tom Sessions, enjoying an
apres drink or two, 2013.

2014 trial run of the new
sit-ski... it rocks!

Shredding the pow with Gil,
2014.

Simon (AKA "Mooney"), Jimmy and me (31). The serious business of post-ski-pre-après photo.

With Tom Sessions when I was 33 not looking at pretty girls in bikinis.

Aged 33, with Garritt (G-dog) on my world tour, he was with me for the entire journey... legend.

With my family on Dad's MBE day.

Aged 33 with Bootham School friends. We're all grown up but essentially the same people.

Big Bad Bike Ride 2014.

Dedicated to the sun and 33.
Two words... Sexy Beast.

Pull ups with
Mark. Date:
every week for
the last ten years.

Kite surfing with Glen in Squamish, British Columbia, Canada.
Summer 2014.

Speaking at the Whistler Waldorf school in Whistler, Canada, 2015.

Zoolander party at Albemarle Road. Everyone looking really really ridiculously good looking as they attempt 'Blue Steel' model pouts.

Aged 34, the very serious business of book writing. Jimmy enjoying a Bloody Mary for bloody inspiration!

suits whilst wearing even more expensive watches. He's far too modest and grounded to talk about his success. However, I know that he spent a night on Table Mountain in South Africa spooning George, so he's fallible. Alex's top quality is that he always makes the time and effort to see his true friends. He turns up to birthday parties and makes no mention of the fact he took an eight-hour flight just to be there. He's more interested in how other people are doing than himself.

Simon: AKA 'Mooney', spent the first half of his life drawing dicks and talking about shagging. He's then spent the second half of his life doing exactly the same, while mountain biking. He's created a pretty radical life for himself doing what he loves, and he chose Whistler in Canada in which to do it – nice move. This has been exceptionally useful for my ski trips. Simon's always thinking of ways to make things easier, more comfortable and, most importantly, faster. He has always had a huge sense of responsibility, loyalty and duty. So, whilst he lives like a kid, he's one of the most grown up people I know. Sadly for him, this has not been in the vertical sense.

Tom: Tom flies, literally. This has been through a steadfast devotion to eating vegetables and practicing Jedi-martial arts (he calls it Tai Chi). A totally cool dude, so cool he married the hottest girl at school, Kate, who's still hot and just had his baby... living the dream. His feet are firmly on the ground and he's my hippy friend who I'm comfortable to call my best friend. He's thoughtful, fun, perceptive and a cool bastard: I love and hate him in equal measure.

Olly: Olly is a school friend who has, in no particular order, started and closed several businesses, drives unfeasibly fast cars, gained and lost several stone, drinks too much, fancies my little sister and idolises my dad. Despite trying his best to be an utter cock, he's actually a wonderful guy. He lives for the moment like nobody I know – high octane, do it now, 'live every day like it's your last'. He frequently finds himself in awkward pickles, which he invariably recounts later to raucous laughter. He has an unrivalled ability to laugh at himself. There's never a dull moment with Ol, my family adore him. Even my sister, and she's way out of his league.

Matty: Matty is the old school friend who instigated the high speed Death Runs across the car park in my first wheelchair. His ability to run fast has waned somewhat over the years, to be replaced by an unhealthy enthusiasm for beer and sausages. So much so that he's dedicated his life to them. He runs his own specialist butchers by day and has the beer at night. Matty was my first friend at Bootham and we've been close ever since. We travelled to Singapore, Malasia and the USA together, as well as numerous other places. Matty's proved to be a ballsy, tenacious and brave man who's always been comfortable with doing what he wants. I really admire that about him.

Jonny: You might remember Jonny from the beginning of this book. He was the classmate I beat at chess. I didn't need to repeat that, but it gives me so much pleasure that I figured I'd mention it again. Luckily he hasn't been crushed by his humiliating defeat. I've known Jonny the longest out of all my friends. His huge brain means he calculates everything, a bit like 'Data' off Star Trek. This makes his advice excellent, it's always calculated and reasoned. His humour is bone-dry and his wife, Claire (also a Bootham girl) is the nicest person you could meet. What she see's in him is a mystery. Maybe it's his ginger hair.

Alastair: 'Ali' is best described as anal. If I didn't make that perfectly clear from the outset he'd be insulted. His mind is extraordinarily large and tidy. Remember how you 'defragmented' your old Windows PC? He does this with his brain on a daily basis. This has led him to a career in IT. He's currently responsible for disseminating the world's events onto The Guardian's web space. He does so using Apple products, a job designed in heaven for him. I can rely on Ali like nobody else. If he says he'll be somewhere at a certain time, he'll be there; he could teach George a thing or two.

The above are all school friends, there are lots more I've met later in life...

Garritt: 'G-Dog' is the six foot three South African I went travelling around the world with. It's the way he understands things that I'm always grateful for. He's one of the few PAs I've had who knows when 'this is Fraser's time' and leaves the room. You rarely see him leave and his ability to appear at the right time is uncanny. He makes 'being me' easier than anyone I've ever known. I've been lucky with those I've met but G-Dog is one of the greatest. I could take the piss out of him here, but he's had his fair share in the book so I'll let him off.

Dylan: Dylan, as I mentioned already, is a unique character. He's a Kiwi who worked for me for about eighteen months before returning to New Zealand. While he would never admit it, he realised his life was more interesting and esoteric in the UK, so he returned for another year in 2014. One of his proudest achievements is staring down the apocalypse in 2012 and personally exposing the suspicious nature of the new world order. He also adores pro-wrestling (yes *that* wrestling) and cricket. He describes himself not as a 'carer' or 'Personal Assistant' but *'life enhancer'*. I probably agree. Despite his eccentricity, he's hugely sensible and the best storyteller I've met. I've yet to meet someone who doesn't like him.

Jegan: Is ice cool and rivals Dylan's laid back attitude. So laid back he frequently drops off the radar. When he crops up he's the same old 'J'. Jegan is a York University friend and, for several years, was my main PA. The icy coolness of this vinyl-spinning, urban-loving man has never waivered. He is extremely thoughtful, and always smiles. Since his degree in Electronics he's become a maths teacher in London, this makes him one of the hardest working and least thanked men in the UK. Jegan earned his respect long ago and now he commands it.

Mark Bednarski: AKA 'Spartacus', was another early PA of mine, first at school and then university. After a successful career as a professional social worker and counsellor, he is now a government investigator responsible for helping those who have suffered injustice. Mark always looks stylish, and his ability to trim extraordinarily tidy sideburns defies belief. He currently sports a beard, every hair of which he has a personal relationship with. Mark is tidy, precise and pragmatic: always seeing how I can tackle obstacles. As a multi-dan black belt in Kung Fu (Wing Chung) he is not to be messed with.

Rory: AKA 'Raul', was one of my first PAs at school. Back then he was a long-haired hippy. Since then, he has transformed himself into a hard-core copper. He is stronger, fitter and faster than the bad guys he catches... dirty criminals. I have had many adventures with Rory, including tours around the USA, Europe and many slightly-seedy bars. One of his proudest achievements is regularly seeing personalised graffiti on the streets of London calling him a c**t. I regard him as *the* funniest man I know, his ability to cut anyone down in one sentence is unsurpassed. In fact, I daren't make a gag about him, as he'll only retort with something way more amusing and witty. Also, I'm a bit scared, as he may chase me down with those stumpy little legs.

Then there's co-author James, 'Jimmy', who is firmly within the Inner Circle. He is mentioned in the foreword of this book so he does not get the chance to edit it. If you have read this far, you will understand our friendship is watertight.

Finally, and most importantly, there's the core of my inner circle, my family. Mum, Dad, Rebecca, Sophie, Lucy. I won't waste words explaining the closeness we have. It's absolute.

My first tier of Inner Circle friends is a much longer list... it probably numbers fifty plus people. You'll notice that the first list is all male, and though hot girls may be welcome, be warned there is some tough competition. This list is less sexist. It's also too long to list fully, but I'll mention a few so that I can make them smile.

Gil: Gil is the ski instructor I've mentioned throughout the book. He's the most advanced instructor in Whistler, which makes him amongst the best in North America and, therefore, the world. To list a few of his skills: he's excellent at looking for ways to improve things, takes absolute responsibility for those he works with, communicates extremely effectively, finds new ways of doing things, is infinitely patient, tolerant and instils trust and mutual respect in absolutely everyone he works with. Above all, he has a need for speed and ability to smash any sit-ski run. It was with Gil that I hit my personal top-speed record. I can't say how fast it was but it was *fast*. You might notice that this list of qualities matches the chapters and themes of this book. I can't describe how absolutely safe I feel when skiing with Gil.

Glen: Glen was an apprentice instructor on the adaptive ski programme when I first visited Whistler and has moved up the ranks. Now one of their core instructors, he was one of the A-Team who took me up Spanky's Ladder. In fact, he contributed the most as he was directly behind the sit-ski to take the weight when others slipped or repositioned themselves. He was the caboose. Following my trip to Canada in the summer of 2014, I can also credit him with introducing me to his other, perhaps main, love – kite-surfing. He's a suave jock, women struggle to keep their clothes on when they see him. Going for drinks with him is always enjoyable...

Mark Bassett: Gym master, personal trainer, life councillor. Mark has made a career of looking after himself and others. He's bloody good at it. His enthusiasm for each gym session has remained undiminished ever since I first asked for help nine years ago. Time and again he's helped me find an area of physical challenge and then expertly discovered a way to develop exercises that push my limits. For the last eight years, this has involved investigating ways of getting my body fit for skiing; core fitness, upper body strength and control, and neck strength. When I reflect on how important skiing has become to me, I can't understate Mark's contribution. He's made the impossible more possible.

Michael: Beefcake, hard-nut, gym addict and good bloke. An Aussie PA that helped make my world trip a reality. Rory is grateful that he has kept on the right side of the law.

Desiree: I met Desiree when she was a volunteer on the Whistler Adaptive Ski Program. She has a smile that is only outshone by her enthusiasm and skills with a camera. Without exception she has made the time to come see me when I'm in Canada and seeing her is always delightful. She laughs at my jokes and has plenty of her own. She's pretty much the perfect babe: intelligent, creative, gorgeous and determined.

Frank: A late addition. Frank is my current main PA. In addition to winning the Edinburgh marathon and representing Scotland internationally, he's also very good at adding structure to my at-home physio and exercise. Typical for a marathon runner, this has been in the areas of stamina and fitness. When we go to the gym, he exercises so furiously that it looks like he's in fast-forward, and a bit like a flapping fish. It's like one stage below having a fit. Others look on like he might need help, but I reassure them that this is quite normal.

Kevin: Physiotherapist, another fitness nut and consummate professional (there's a weird theme developing here which I hadn't noticed!). You can ask him anything about anything and he'll give you detailed dossier; the history of the Russian Tsars, the development of the Rwandan state or a peculiar pain behind my right knee.

Gill: Physiotherapist, 'Gill Fizz', she became my physio when I was twelve. She's an expert and drop dead gorgeous. She regularly puts me through what I describe as 'a world of pain', but good pain. She's basically a member of our family.

Becky: Becky is a lawyer with a big brain who is incredibly well read. I'm a bit of geek when it comes to the stuff of politics and I enjoy talking about it with people... the challenge is finding somebody to talk to! Becky also has the endearing quality of always caring for others. She knows and enjoys the art of conversation. So, not only does she tolerate my chat, she has the uncanny ability to appear genuinely interested.

Riva: Jimmy and I met Riva when she was working as a management apprentice for the Whistler Adaptive Ski Program. Although that career option didn't take off for her, she has remained a close friend and has since become a teacher. She's the lady who sets up the school assembly presentations I give in Whistler. I had the pleasure of seeing her in the summer of 2014 when I returned to Canada for what was the first, but not last, non-skiing-based trip there. Riva is one of the tallest girls I know. Luckily for Dylan, she's not hight-ist – they are currently an item.

Chris: Another late entry. Having just returned from Whistler in 2015, I can credit a large part of my enjoyment to him. He's a successful entrepreneur and, these days, chooses to use his time to teach adaptive ski instruction. What he proved incredibly good at is 'how' thinking. Without geeking out too much on the details, let me just say he took a fresh approach to my sit-skiing and the process was thrilling. He also likes to go extremely fast, so obviously it doesn't hurt to butter him up a bit here for the purpose of future ski trips.

So, there you have it, my somewhat amorphous (and evolving) inner circles.

In addition to illustrating the wide variety of those I've put my trust in, this section was intended to offer a high-five to them, to get their names in print and say 'thanks'.

As Jimmy and I discussed who we'd write about, we soon realised there were far too many to include. This may sound like a massive cliché but it's been a humbling process. I imagine it's similar to deciding whom to invite to a wedding – so many people, so few places. But I've had to draw a line and move on. So, if you're not here, don't fret, you're loved.

What ties all these people together is that I trust them. If I could've written a one-chapter book, this would be the one

I'd have chosen to write. My inner circle know everything; it means we can all talk freely about things. The first tier allows me to be the best guy I can be from the support the Inner Circle gives me. My hand has been forced in life, as I *have* to trust others a great deal in order to get stuff done. If I didn't I'd be absolutely stuck. Like everyone, my foundation of trust began with my mum when I was born, and like many other fortunate people she is my still bedrock.

On the whole, I suspect most people would benefit from putting their trust in others more than they do. When I talk about this with friends they often cite an event in their past where their trust in someone was broken and since then they find trusting others difficult. Typically, this is in relationships, but it also includes all sorts of situations – work, family, friendships etc. This has happened to me too, it's normal, shit happens. I absolutely *have* to get over these things and continue to put my trust in others. What I can report is that it's a good way to go. Overcoming the disappointments has opened up a really interesting and enjoyable life.

A good example here, is in the gym. Mark figured a way for me to do pull-ups. He lifts me into position and then I do as much as I can. When I started I was contributing about 20% to each repetition. Mark's a beefcake so was probably grateful for the opportunity to squeeze out a few reps with a client. Now, though, it's well past 70% and, on a good day, I'm pulling over 85% of my weight. Yes, I've got stronger, yes, I do more of the lifting, but Mark makes it possible – it's our collaborative approach that made it happen. If I tried to do it myself, I'd have failed completely and contributed 0% because I wouldn't have bothered. Crucial to this is knowing that when I lose my grip, which happens, I have absolute trust in Mark. It's this trust that makes the thing happen.

As I've tried to explain, I've found that the best way to create trust is by taking responsibility, so when things do go wrong I've got the attitude that won't compromise the trust. Taking responsibility allows me to garner trust from others and helps them to accept mine. It forms the strong friendships, which makes everything happen. Thus, friendship is something I truly value. The value of turning to and trusting my friends is, as you've seen, a lesson I learnt early in life. It's just taken me a while to understand it. Writing this book has taken it to a whole new level.

It's worth clarifying the important differences between responsibility, causality, liability and rules of the game. The strategy of taking absolute responsibility isn't the solution to everything. It's a perspective that, more often than not, helps me deal with problems. Even better, it makes for a happier and more fulfilling life. The interplay between responsibility and liability is one I find interesting. Put as briefly as possible, if everyone takes more responsibility for their actions, then friction and problems caused by blaming others (causality and liability) dissipates. From my perspective, the world would benefit if more people took more responsibility for their actions, rather than blaming others. The trend-line, however, seems to be in the opposite direction.

Honesty is a prerequisite in any decent relationship, particularly with me. I've got to be honest about where my boundaries are. I'm comfortable pushing my limits but it's my responsibility to know where the line is. Although I've made mistakes here; skiing crash and paragliding crash, bad girl chat *inter alia*. It's the collaboration with others that's been my saviour. I've learnt that real achievements are only possible with huge degrees of trust and collaboration.

This book is testament to the trust I have in Jimmy to help

me write it. In fact I take that back, we *co*-wrote it. Hopefully, what comes out of it is that I could never have written it myself. This is not because I can't type, it's because Jimmy has provided much of the framework and perspectives that have extracted so much from me. It's important to be clear that what I have shared in this book *are* my perspectives. Writing it with Jimmy has helped me enormously, but this is because Jimmy's perspectives have been informed by our friendship. We see things extraordinarily similarly, because we've formed our models of the world together. At times, he knows me better than I know myself and he freely admits to being more reliant on me for clarification on himself! I'd like to think he couldn't do it on his own either (his stories are not as good!). By doing it this way we've used both our skills and hope we've produced a better book.

This book is neither original nor does it pretend to be a blueprint. It's just a particular viewpoint: how I respond to problems. I hope you've enjoyed me sharing it.

I'm reminded of an interview with Andy Murray, the tennis ace. He was asked whether his greatest achievement was winning the men's singles at Wimbledon or winning the Olympic Gold Medal with Team GB. His answer was words to the effect of, "I think I'd have to go with the Olympics. Wimbledon is personal, Olympics is a team thing. That's the greater achievement."

Of course, you can have *personal* achievements! I have mine. However, when you're part of something involving others, the achievement becomes orders of magnitude greater. It's not a one-sided equation, it's a dance of sorts. The more you dance the more fun it is. Friendships, marriages, families, work, sports – *everything* in fact.

I've been very careful not to preach in this book. But if I was to dare to offer some actual advice, I suppose now's the time.

Dance more everyone. If I can, you can.

Afterword from Fraser

Hello again. This is being written immediately after writing the foreword, so it's intended to be a continuation of sorts. Only now you've read the book.

I hope you can see that I wasn't joking when I said it made me think.

Now that we're here, I can also tell you that the team we created – Jimmy, Lisa, and me – have spent a good part of the last few months killing ourselves with laughter. This was during our final (final!) edit read-through. Mostly, this was with all three of us together in the same room. But often one of us was on the other side of the world. Regardless, these sessions were a serious and reliable source of laughs that neither Jimmy nor I saw coming. Lisa, because she's Lisa, probably did.

The source of this laughter generally focussed around mine and Jimmy's terrible misuse and abuse of the English language. When presenting Lisa with a section that we felt made perfect sense, the actual semantics of our words would frequently send Lisa into tears of laughter, while Jimmy and I looked at one another in bemusement (wondering what all the fuss was about). A decent example was during the 'bravery' section you read. We looked up definitions of bravery in dictionaries. In our first draft, we described this process as 'looking *at* dictionaries'. Lisa, after regaining her composure, said that the way we'd put it sounded like we just went and looked at a wall of dictionaries. That we didn't *open* them, we just looked *at* them wondering what bravery means. Luckily, we've got a good enough sense of humour to see how crazy this sounded. If we hadn't, the editing process would have been a punishing experience! Lisa is currently using this story as a source of guaranteed laughs at dinner parties with her literary friends – Jimmy and I are pleased to be of assistance. This sort of gaff happened about once a page, sometimes twice, that's been a lot of laughs for us all.

The book project has also given me the opportunity to look at myself more objectively, to better understand how I do things. I've realised I'm better at 'walking the walk' not 'talking the talk'.

For example, the benefit of absorbing blame for my ski crashes and taking responsibility for things, weren't necessarily things I did consciously, it's just what I did. This is different from being 'honest with myself', it's been about waking up to what I was doing anyway. Some of my habits were benefiting me and some of them certainly weren't, and probably still aren't in places. Getting them clear in my own mind and out on paper was, at times, a process of gruelling extraction, rather than something that was bursting out of me. But, it's made me better able to deal with things.

The *process* we created to write this is what gave me the chance to look at myself from this abstracted perspective. Not somebody else's, but an abstracted position of my own. The chapter structure helped a great deal in this respect. The theme was laid in front of me when Jimmy and I set the chapters and the content we needed to find to fill them. To this extent, I now know that Jimmy had a better idea of where we were headed than I did at the time. This was probably why the process was so fraught at the beginning. Nevertheless, I get it.

Mum says Jimmy's the brother I never had. I don't think this is entirely right, I think we get on better than any brothers I've met. We've never had a meaningful argument or disagreement, not even in writing this book. If it's possible, we now know each other even better.

So, while I'll continue to rely on him to talk about everything and nothing – friendship, relationships, work, health, my current hairstyle and wardrobe choices – I'll miss the talks we had in producing this book. It took thirty years to live enough to write it and about two years for Jimmy to persuade me to. Once we got into it, I became a bit desperate because, it's taken six months to a year longer than I thought it would. But, now it's here and I'm pleased that I've done it. Even the best parties have to end.

Another thing, the timing of this book is proving excellent too. As we are finishing it, I'm bouncing in and out of what I might reflect on being some pretty serious Dark Times. This book is the kind of book I need to read right now, so its advice is something I intend to embrace. 'I've Decided' this isn't the end of a process, it's the beginning of a new one. I've some interesting new goals that I'd like to pursue, and most of them leverage from the process of writing this book.

The obvious question is whether I'd like to write another one. The problem is that we've no material left. Time for some more adventures. I've also held a couple of stories back, but believe me, you ain't hearing those (Only joking Grandma). Another consideration is Jimmy's liver as, generally speaking, he'd write most prodigiously when consuming Bloody Marys. He'd hit a sweet spot, knock out a few thousand words and then, inevitably, everything would go a little surreal and he'd realise it was time to stop for the day. His mind can be an odd place at times, and his liver can only take so much. I think writing this book has made me a better person and most of that has been due to Jimmy and for this I will be forever grateful. In fact, James is the *only* person I could have written this book with! So, if you think I'm a dick having read my book, Jimmy's reputation will suffer.

But, for now, thanks for reading it. Next time we speak, I really hope I know who you are. If you hear some familiar lines and I start saying 'definitely' a lot, please just take the time to explain to me who you are. I don't need to play these games with you, as you're now in my Outer Inner Circle.

References:

Davis, R. (2013) 'Adrian Leftwich, The Unforgiven' (Johannesburg, Daily Maverick, 22 April, 2013). http://www. dailymaverick.co.za/article/2013-04-22-adrian-leftwich-the-unforgiven/#.VRu5YkYgrm5

Hogg, S. (2013) 'Tribute to Adrian: 1940 -2013' (Birmingham, Development Leadership Program (DLP), April, 2013). http://www.dlprog.org/about-us/adrian-leftwich/tribute-to-adrian.php

Leftwich, A. (2002) 'I Gave The Names' (London, Granta, June 15, 2002). Issue 78, ref #182892, pp 11 to 31.

Leftwich, A. (ed.) (2004) *What Is Politics?*, 2nd edn (Cambridge, Polity).

Leftwich, A. and Hogg, S. (2008) 'The Politics of Institutional Indigenization: Leaders, Elites and Coalitions in building appropriate and legitimate institutions for sustainable growth and social development' (Birmingham, Development Leadership Program (DLP), January, 2008). http://publications.dlprog.org/The%20Politics%20of%20 Institutional%20Indigenization.pdf

Notes from the back cover artist
Steve Hopkins

Fraser and James approached me for the cover art after seeing other examples of my work. As Fraser described the project to me, I was more or less instantly producing a piece to support it in my head. I like to hide stuff in my art for the viewer to discover. Fraser and James asked me to share a few with you to give you an idea of where I was coming from. Here are a some notes:

Location: Where else but in the mountains? Lofty location, lofty ambitions, a high-flyer amongst them.

Fraser deals with a fair bit of uncertainty in life which puts an urgency into the way he goes about things – screw it, just do it. So he's leaping off a cliff, the bomb fuse is lit, no time to waste, no time to dwell, do it now. Fraser radiates 'make the most of it, keep positive'; like fire, it's a warm glow that brings joy and others to him. But it's hot so he's got to keep moving or it'll consume him, he keeps those flames streaking behind him as he takes off into the unknown.

Carefree, yes. Careless, no way. He's got that paragliding parachute behind him, like his ski instructor's arms, there to make the ride an enjoyable one; in fact, they're coming off that cliff too.

Life's ups and downs are represented by the arrows you'll see dotted around. But screw the landscape, Fraser doesn't let them tell him which way to go, that's HIS decision, and he's bloody well DECIDED, he's jumping, who's coming?!

[Steve is available for commissions and can be contacted on hops_artist@gmail.com]

Biographies

Fraser Kennedy
After studying Politics to Master's level, Fraser became a Researcher for the Developmental Leadership Program. This is an international research initiative that explores how leadership, power and political processes drive or block successful development. While a York resident all his adult life, he can frequently be found elsewhere, more often than not in Canada, where he likes to ski. Fraser can be contacted at: fraser@fraser.kennedy.com. If you'd like to make a donation to help him buy his new sit-ski, please contact him.

James Waggott
James is a California-born Yorkshireman. Following a career in marketing, he became an entrepreneur. Current projects include French luxury tourism, social enterprise, guest lecturing on enterprise, and others. www.boutiquebargecompany.com, www.jameswaggott.com, www.smart-aid.co.uk.
James can be contacted at: james@jameswaggott.com

Lisa Chaney
Lisa Chaney has lectured and tutored in the history of art and literature, made TV and radio broadcasts, and reviewed and written for journals and newspapers, including The Sunday Times, the Spectator and the Guardian. She much enjoys mentoring other writers and also the hard graft, cooperation and thought-provoking ideas involved in editing. She is the author of three best-selling biographies on: Elizabeth David, J.M. Barrie and, most recently, Coco Chanel, called An Intimate Life. www.lisachaney.com